# I'd Rather Not

## ROBERT SKINNER

STEER
FORTH
PRESS

LEBANON, NEW HAMPSHIRE

First published in Australia in 2023 by Black Inc.,
an imprint of Schwartz Books Pty Ltd.

For information about permission to reproduce
selections from this book, write to:
Steerforth Press L.L.C., 31 Hanover Street, Suite 1
Lebanon, New Hampshire 03766

Cataloging-in-Publication Data is available from the Library of Congress

ISBN 978-1-58642-378-0

The phrase 'misery of democracy' (p. 21) is from Donald Barthelme's story 'I Bought a Little City'; 'banging on the gates of Australian literature' (p. 25) bastardises the closing lines of Richard Brautigan's story '1/3 1/3 1/3'; the chapter 'Always Coming Home' (p. 107) takes its title from Ursula K. Le Guin's novel of the same name.

Grateful acknowledgement is made to *The Monthly*, in which many of this book's chapters first appeared, in different forms, and to the estate of Adrienne Rich for permission to reproduce a passage from the poem 'Sources' (p. ix).

Printed in the United States of America

*In memory of Harriet McKnight*
*and Benjamin Leske*

# Contents

No person, trying to take responsibility for her or his identity, should have to be so alone. There must be those among whom we can sit down and weep, and still be counted as warriors.

—ADRIENNE RICH

I have never been lost, but I was bewildered once for three days.

—DANIEL BOONE

# PART
# ONE

# 1

## War and Peace

I retired when I was twenty-eight years old, but ran out of money the same afternoon, so I caught a bus to the dole office. My feeling about unemployment was: *Someone's* gotta do it. Why not me? The pay was lousy, but I'd heard the hours were good.

I had been working for the past sixteen years – driving buses, washing dishes, picking grapes, packing boxes, building exhibitions and, once, digging the same trench for three days before someone told me I was digging in the wrong direction. (Subconsciously, I think, I'd started digging for home.) I was fed up with the whole racket.

At the Centrelink office I learnt that it was no longer called 'the dole'. Some overpaid marketing agency had rebranded it 'Newstart'. The walls were covered with inspirational posters ('When opportunity knocks, open the door!') alongside more practical advice, telling us not to drink alcohol before job interviews. Fake nails clacked away at keyboards. Someone called my name, and I followed him into a small room. I hadn't even sat down before he started trying to sign me up for forklift-driving jobs on the other side of town.

'Whoa,' I said. 'This isn't the kind of Newstart I had in mind at *all.'*

I had only just moved to Melbourne. It was a place filled with magic and possibility. I wanted to meet interesting people at rooftop bars. I wanted to read Russian novels. What I didn't want was a pesky job, but try telling that to your dole officer.

'Listen,' I said, 'our economy seems to rely on a 5 per cent unemployment rate. Can't I just be one of those 5 per cent for a while?'

The long answer was no.

People, I've found, want you to be busy. They don't require you to contribute anything meaningful, otherwise how do you explain professions like 'consulting'? They just want you to be busy. Genghis Khan could move into your street and people would say, 'Well, at least he's *working.'*

My dole officer changed tack. He straightened his tie and wafted some cologne in my direction.

'What about truck driving?' he said. 'I've got some great truck-driving jobs.'

I'd spent the previous three years driving tour buses in the outback. One morning it had been so hot that I'd woken up with a lisp. I had a crooked back and still harboured some latent racism (mostly against the Swiss) that I was trying to deal with. I was sick of driving. But you can't just come out and say that.

'What sort of loads would I be carrying? I'm allergic to peanuts.'

'Furniture,' he said, eyeing me suspiciously. 'No peanuts.'

I held in my lap my talismanic copy of *War and Peace*. I had vowed not to get a job until I finished reading it. But the dole officer had obviously sworn some oath of his own. He was so dogged, I was amazed he hadn't risen through the ranks yet.

'Is it far away?' I asked, eventually.

'Just around the corner.'

'Oh. That could make things difficult.'

'Difficult how?'

'Well, I was thinking of moving.'

*

What followed was a series of long and glorious autumn days. I wandered through parks, winked at old ladies and had long boozy dinners in friends' backyards.

My uncle was in town one day, and I explained that, what with the demands of *War and Peace* and everything else going on, I scarcely had time for a job.

'Well, it's a question of priorities, Robbie,' he said.

We looked at each other and I hit the table with my fist. 'Exactly.'

When my second appointment came around, the dole officer asked me how I was getting on, and I told him about the projects I was working on. He made a few notes.

'So, you're writing a book?'

'I'm *reading* a book.'

He became businesslike. He said that, per regulations, I was to start filling out a job diary and applying for twenty jobs a fortnight. Twenty!

It was even more odious than having a job. It sounded like I would be doing a lot of extra work, so I asked if I'd be getting a corresponding pay rise.

His answer was long and wearisome, like your primary school teacher going on and on about not eating pencil shavings.

Eventually I pointed at the job diary and said, 'But. But what's the point of it?'

The point was 'How dare you!' The point was 'We the taxpayers!' etc.

Andy, my friend and housemate, had little sympathy. 'They pay you $230 a week for doing nothing.'

'*I* don't get the money,' I said. 'Our landlord gets it.'

'Oh, not this again.'

'Well, I work just as hard as he does.'

'Not today you didn't.'

'It's a Saturday, Andy. Jesus.'

'Not yesterday, either. You spent all morning trying to glue your boot back together.'

'Okay, so we happen to have a particularly hardworking landlord. But morally ... '

\*

You have three months, by my calculations, to explore a city before your sense of wonder turns to familiarity. I used to board trams with excitement, thinking, *Where will I possibly end up?* Now I knew exactly where.

As the days shortened, the trams ploughed the same old furrows up and back, and I rode with them.

The pay, I was learning, was barely enough to make rent, let alone have the wild times that welfare recipients are always having on the news. And not even the hours were good! There were meetings, job diaries, and you were constantly having to catch two buses out to Broadmeadows, and back again, to attend some forty-five-minute course on Time Management. It's hard to understand what all this was in aid of, but the flourishing of the human spirit was not one of those things.

It began to feel like serving out a sentence, but for how long and for what crime it was hard to say. My reading was turning frequently into napping. I was languishing somewhere between war and peace.

Then, through a series of clerical errors and misunderstandings, I accidentally got a job as a dishwasher.

Every time I start a new dishwashing job, I can't imagine why I ever quit. It's exhilarating. You feel like a general marshalling troops. Waiters pile up coffee cups and teaspoons on one side, chefs drop hot pots and pans into the sink on the other, and you're in the middle of it all, suds flying. At the end of a shift you have that physical tiredness that feels almost like a life well lived. On your lunch break, if you get one, you send out group text messages: 'Friends! You were right! Maybe this *is* the answer!'

And then, after two or three shifts, you start to remember. The sinks are always too low, so you stoop all day, or all night, and wake up in the mornings, or afternoons, with a cracking headache. You get covered face to feet in grime. The kitchens are hot, cramped and almost always an insufferable boys' club. If you're new they'll send you off to fetch a made-up item, like a 'rice peeler' or a 'bucket of steam'. (I would pretend to fall for that one and sit in the storage room reading a book until someone came looking for me.)

You become increasingly convinced that, in the world outside your kitchen, in some endless dusk, bands are playing on street corners, friends are having wild picnics and everyone you like is sleeping with someone else.

It becomes harder and harder to contain the long, loud bouts of moaning at the helpless purgatory of it all. And shift after shift the dishes keep coming. You could work fifteen years in that job and still have nothing to show for it. If you left the sink for one minute to accept your Golden Tea Towel Award, by the time you turned back the sink would be piled with dirties again. Worse, *they're the same dishes.*

And dishes are as good as it gets, by the way. You need a biology degree to remove the oily film that clings to the inside of plastic containers. I had one, but for the wage I was getting I refused to use it. Sometimes I just threw dishes into the bin.

What sort of answer is this to the question of what to do with our short time on Planet Earth? Sometimes I would find myself standing at the sink with my hands dangling in the dirty water, thinking, *This is it. I can't go on. It's just too pointless.* And dishwashing is one of the important jobs! Imagine how the consultants feel!

As soon as I smelt spring in the air, I quit the dishwashing and raced back to the dole office.

Somehow, impossibly, this dole officer was even more cunning than the last one. Within ten minutes I was checkmated. He had the perfect job for me, he said. I didn't understand all the details, but it sounded like I'd be working for a company that couldn't afford a forklift and was settling for me instead. I mumbled something about low blood-sugar levels and pulled some roast chicken out of my bag. (Not all victories can be won with dignity.) I wolfed it down and then pretended to choke on a bone. I writhed around on the ground, clutching my throat. The dole officer sighed, stood up and said, 'We're done for the day.' The man was no fool; he knew a piece of chicken breast when he saw one.

But also, it was 4.30 on a Friday afternoon. I lunged for the door. Not even the best dole officer in the land could catch me before Monday morning. I burst onto the street and sunshine hit me in the eyes as on the day of one's birth. I did something similar to a yodel. I had two more days! Two more days in this world where, right now, a wheeling, chattering flock of rainbow lorikeets was shitting on someone's scooter with what looked like pure joy. Two more days in this world where people play the bassoon, climb trees and help baby turtles get from their nest to the sea; where it's possible to meet someone with whom to spend a lifetime watching wrinkles gather around each other's smiling eyes. Two more days, *at least*, before the vice clamped down on me once more.

# The Perfect Host

The first time I attended one of Manoli's parties was around the time of the global financial crisis. I remember him smashing out the lights of his own bedroom so that we might 'dance more freely', which we appreciated, given those turbulent times. He was the perfect host for the occasion: attentive, entertaining and drunker than anyone else in the room.

One of Manoli's guiding principles is that a party must always have a theme. For those attending, that means suffering the tyranny of dressing up. The light-smashing party was called 'The Recession Party' (or, taking inspiration from Paul Keating, 'The Party We Had To Have'). I remember a lot of pleased-looking lawyers wearing grey beanies and fingerless gloves. At the time I was against the whole business of dressing up, so I wore my regular outfit. But given the condition of my wardrobe in those days, I blended right in. Other guests kept slapping me on the back and saying, 'That's the spirit.'

I used to complain, 'Can't we just drink heavily together?' But it's true, a theme provides a sense of occasion. And by asking guests to don a costume you're soliciting from them a genuine commitment to the party. No one's showing up dressed as a pavlova and pretending they have some place better to be.

Even great parties have awkward beginnings: three people trying to be a crowd in an otherwise empty room and a host trying to quell the terror that no one will arrive. When more guests *do* arrive, they're always in impossible combinations: your Aunty Fran from out of town, the bong-smoking Marxist from next door and the overseas basketball player whom you met on the tram that morning and promised a good time.

At a Manoli-hosted party, guests usually have to wait for him to make his entrance – fashionably late. He sweeps in through the front door wearing some floor-to-ceiling gown, gestures grandly across the room and in his booming baritone says, 'Ladies and gentlemen, have you noticed the dips?' He elevates the business of dressing up to an art form, and embodies another of his golden rules: as the host, you must always set the example for how to party. (Or, as he puts it, 'You should always be the first person to start smashing stuff.')

On arrival, the guests should on no account be able to see the whole party with one sweep of the eyes. Separate rooms are ideal, or partitions at least. It is important that guests can retain, for as long as possible, the hope that they might meet a soulmate, even if the party is populated entirely by real estate agents. There's no need to disappoint them at the door.

Social interaction is laborious at the start of any party. The host's role is to provide a gentle heat, so that people in the room, like particles in a beaker, become energised enough to start reacting. Manoli is more of a centrepiece than a conversationalist, but he still brings people together – the way, say, fireworks might. Or a car crash. And as the house starts filling with friends, strangers and love interests, a party finds its second gear. Everyone becomes charming at the same time. Dancing seems possible. You can tumble easily into conversations, into arms. A good party feels like a rich life, which is presumably why we throw them.

There are people who would be content with an evening like this, who would speak for days about what a lovely party it was, about how they saw Aunty Fran and your neighbour discussing crochet patterns, and how that basketball player couldn't stop smiling, just kept towering over everyone and telling them what a good time he was having.

But a party has a third gear too. What might be referred to as 'getting carried away'. It is the moment when widely held social conventions are abandoned and a party conga-lines onwards according to its own logic. Everything that happens in the third gear – the armpit licking, the couch racing, the String Cheese Incident – makes perfect sense in the context of the party and nowhere else. If your 2 a.m. self went back in time and tried to explain to your 8 p.m. self what the party had descended into, your 8 p.m. self would have a hard time understanding how it had all gone so wrong. Though, if you've been to enough parties, your questions are likely to be logistical rather than philosophical: 'But where did the wedding cake come from?' or 'Why did the possums only bite that one guy?'

In the early days of our short-story magazine, *The Canary Press*, we recruited Manoli to direct our launch parties. He insisted that each issue be presented with a big reveal. 'People deserve a show,' he'd say, and we often went to painful lengths to make this happen.

By the launch of Issue 3, he had already performed as a giant stork, his own mother, Mr and Mrs Shakespeare, and the back end of a pantomime horse. We were getting short on ideas. There was a popular photo of Manoli going around at the time, titled 'Man Reading in Desert'. He was in the outback somewhere, half-naked, hair in Princess Leia buns, reading a copy of Issue 2. So for our Issue 3 launch party we wheeled him out in a giant pool of jelly and said, 'Ladies and gentlemen, we are thrilled to present our follow-up: "Man Reading in Dessert"!' Manoli was sitting in the jelly, wearing bathers and a scuba mask, and reading a hitherto unseen copy of Issue 3. The crowd went wild with confusion. The idea was that everyone would rush forward, throw their money into the jelly and fish out a copy from somewhere near Manoli's legs. No one thought to ask how this might affect sales.

Though it's hardly on the scale of raising barns or building orphanages, a party provides the opportunity to bring people together, briefly, in one unifying moment, before we all return to our lonely homes. At a house party, we wanted to see how many people we could bring together in our kitchen, which even our landlord had described as 'kinda poky'. There were fifty-eight of us in a room the size of most people's bathrooms. People tried to pass around drinks. Someone gave a speech. Manoli found himself up near the kitchen shelf, from where he started handing down strands of saffron like a Babylonian king. From inside the mass of bodies, one of our more responsible housemates yelled, 'Manoli, you're blowing our whole budget! You wouldn't even let me buy *hummus*!'

The withholding of the hummus was in accordance with Manoli's theory that you want to keep people slightly on edge and hungry with desire. Food only quells the revolutionary spirit. This was hard for him, given the ancestral weight of Greek tradition, its thousands of years of hospitality. 'It pains me,' he said. But the evidence on the morning after suggested that people made do: a jar of Vegemite with a spoon in it, beer coasters covered in barbecue sauce and bite marks.

For one launch I bought a dozen bottles of champagne, hoping to make a dignified toast. But it was only much later, once the party was in full swing, that we remembered our plan. 'The toast!' we cried. By then the bar was in disarray, and people who wanted a drink were being sent back into the crowd to find an empty glass or mug. So Manoli and I weaved through the crowd with the champagne, pouring it straight into the mouths of friends, comrades and eminent literary figures. In between, I took swigs, to reassure everyone that all was safe and above board. It wasn't quite the sophisticated moment we had imagined, but at the time it was hard to imagine a greater pleasure than that unholy communion. I must have swigged a little too hard in my excitement, because someone stopped me in my travels and said, 'Mate, you are bleeding *profusely.*'

Where does a party go from here? Down, usually. Like the fall of Rome. Those people with lives to go back to will stagger home, or pair off and tumble into the sheets. The morning after the jelly episode, Manoli went interstate and I was left with the clean-up job. While I trudged around picking up bottles and pulling down streamers, I had the sensation of being watched, that bad news was lurking for me somewhere like a lion in the long grass. And then I saw the pool of jelly.

We had purchased the jelly powder from a professional jelly wrestler. To turn it into jelly proper, all we had to do was fill our blow-up pool with water and stir it in. 'Keep going!' my treacherous colleagues had cried, as I'd directed the hose from the laundry tap. 'More! More!' We'd made that jelly with such wanton enthusiasm. The next day, standing over the pool and its gloopy contents, I had the same feeling that one might have on the morning after a coup: a distinct cooling of passions and a mounting sense of responsibility.

The jelly and I were on the first floor. The only way to get rid of it was to carry all 300 litres downstairs by the bucketload. Once outside, I lumbered onto the street and tipped it into the drain. The jelly wrestler had assured us it was biodegradable, but who the hell knows? Hunched over and pouring out the red sludge, I looked as if I was committing if not a homicidal crime then at least an environmental one. A few bedraggled copies of Issue 3 tumbled out with the jelly as young families watched in disgust from the cafe across the road.

With the right company, though, mornings after a party can be immensely pleasurable. People emerge, hungover, to piece together the night before. I imagine this is what old age might feel like, if you're lucky, and you've managed to live well: connecting aches and pains to fondly remembered events; trading stories with your closest friends; feeling the sun on your face, the rumble of the stereo; pottering around the house for a while and, finally, out to lunch.

# Cinderella Pays the Rent

The main problem with my living arrangements was that I hadn't made any. As we loaded my things into a rental van, my housemate asked, 'Where to now?'

I waved a hand. 'Oh, it always works out.'

I was still in the short-story business, which was going great in every respect except the financial ones. I dropped my things in our office and moved into my friend Alex's shed.

If you find yourself sleeping on the floor of a shed, it's easy to believe you're in the early stages of greatness, rather than just going badly. As a society, we are in love with the Cinderella story. At nights, I lay on the grease-stained carpet as the wind whipped in and under the door, waiting for the ol' upswing in my fortunes, thinking, *Any moment now.*

Then, surprisingly, improbably, things got slightly worse.

My friend Alex sat me down in the kitchen to tell me he was moving out of the share house and into an apartment with his girlfriend.

'Does it have a shed?'

It did not.

\*

'The best way to become a millionaire,' said my dad, 'is to start with a billion and work your way down.' For various reasons this hadn't panned out. I spent the rest of the year sleeping on couches, lawns and living room floors. When I ran out of friends to call on for favours, I started carrying my swag to the local cricket club/dog park. The plan was to funnel leftover rent money into the magazine.

I was sleeping in what might reasonably be described as a ditch, though I tried not to think of it in those terms for morale reasons. I was laid out on a flat strip of ground under the spreading branches of a tree, between a wooden fence line and a grassy hillock that more or less shielded me from view.

On my first night I woke up thirsty in the middle of the night and went padding off barefoot, looking for a drink. There were no drinking fountains, so I hopped the fence into someone's yard and drank straight from a garden hose under a big, boisterous moon that no one else was around to see. I felt the thrill that night of standing, very briefly, on the edge of civilisation.

In the mornings I'd roll up my swag, hoick my things onto my back and scuttle off like a crab to avoid being seen. Once that initial indignity was over, I blended in with the citizenry. I'd stop off at a local cafe, brush my teeth, drink a coffee, read a few poems. Then I'd cycle to our office, where we spent all day banging on the gates of Australian literature.

*

There are all sorts of barriers stopping people getting to the top. It's interesting to consider how much energy goes into stopping people sneaking out the bottom way. We install spikes under bridges (as one might do against pigeons), build impossible-to-sleep-upon benches and pay police to move people on from whatever safe and dry place they've found.

My own problems were of the canine variety.

I had been sleeping at the cricket club on and off for most of the summer. There had been some unfortunate moments – like the night I was swarmed by mosquitoes, or the night I had drinks with a yoga instructor and it seemed to be going well because she leaned forward, gave me a look and said, 'So ... where do you live, Robert?' and, not wanting to get into *that* whole situation, I described at length the bucolic scenes and green vistas of the cricket club while remaining vague on the details of my vantage point, so that, later, when I suggested we go back to her place, she was so taken by my description of the view that she insisted we go back to mine. But overall, it hadn't been such a terrible time.

On most nights I lay under the spreading branches of a tree, preoccupied with the business of running a short-story magazine. Better to sleep on hard ground with a sense of purpose, I thought, than in eiderdown without one.

On the first day of autumn, I was invited to a literary gala. I knew it was autumn because I woke up covered in leaves. I collected my suit from our office, and rode into town to meet our copyeditor, Kate. In the Treasury Gardens that evening, we drank prosecco and ate salmon cakes. Ministers gave speeches in marquees. We tried hobnobbing, and then gave it up to focus on the drinking. At midnight, I wobbled home drunk on my bike to resume my residence at the cricket club.

The next morning, I awoke groggy and hungover. My head hurt. My body felt like it had landed in a sleeping position from a height of thirty feet. Strange noises were coming from outside my swag. With great trepidation I peeked out. A beagle was pacing around in a state of agitation. She obviously thought that something worse than a hangover had befallen me, because she was pawing at the ground and whining anxiously. I tried to give her a thumbs up, but it can't have been a convincing one because she sat straight down and started sending out high-pitched distress signals. This dog was going to ruin everything. I tried to shoo her away with a back issue I kept handy, and the beagle lost her mind. She let loose with crazed and horrified barks that brought people running from everywhere.

In a panic, I started bundling up my things. I made for the park gates, trailing clothes and blankets. Faces appeared on the ridge. As I ran, I half-turned and shouted something to the effect of, 'Please buy our magazine!'

I say this with sincerity: those were the days. When you're so passionate about something that you barely care where you sleep.

*

Two years later I was homeless again and sleeping in the back of a van. This time there was no magazine, no great mission. I was just sort of lying there without a house.

On my first night in the van, I felt a familiar exhilaration: *Ha ha, they'll never find me here!* But this time it was followed by: *How will anyone find me?*

One night I spent six hours driving around Brunswick looking for a park outside a place with free wifi so I could download *When Harry Met Sally* on my laptop, and I thought: *What if it's just this, forever?*

I crawled into the back of the van and read a sweet, trusty book by the glow of a head torch whose batteries would die in the middle of the night. That's where I was, fast asleep, when someone broke in.

When I came to, I could feel a draught coming through an open door. Torchlight bounced around nightmarishly in the front of the van. Someone was rifling through the things on the passenger seat and

reciting its contents to an accomplice behind him.
I woke up because I heard him say, 'Banana.'

I yelled, 'HEY!'

I bellowed it, like a madman trying to shake himself loose from a bad dream.

The two thieves bolted. I jumped into the front of the van, pulled the door shut, and saw them streaking through the night. Blood was roaring in my ears. The van was no longer a sanctuary. It felt like there were no safe places left on Earth.

I started the engine and swung out of the parking spot. I thought that I'd have to go after them, maybe run one of them down, that there'd be no peace for any of us until one of us was dead.

They had run out of the cul-de-sac and onto the main road, but I didn't know where, or which way I should go. I flicked on the headlights.

The dashboard clock showed 1.34 a.m. I sat for a while with the wipers going, watching through the windscreen at the only way in and out of the street.

And eventually, for lack of a better idea, I ate the banana.

# 4

# Lessons from Camels

For reasons that are still unclear to me, I agreed to go on a ten-day camel trek with my parents. When they invited me my initial reaction was, *I've got a whole LIFE going on here, I can't just take off.* I had a pile of junk mail to read and some pretty firm dinner plans. A few weeks later I was at a party where I didn't think much of the people. Or, more accurately, I didn't think the people thought much of me. So I wandered outside, thought, *Phooey to you, city living,* and texted my parents. 'I'm in.'

A week before departure they called me from Adelaide, huddled together and shouting into the speakerphone.

'When you get here, we need you to pick up

30 kilograms of potatoes. We're in charge of the potatoes.'

'Don't stress him out,' said my mum. 'You just bring yourself.'

'Yeah, yeah, but just – and the potatoes.'

My dad explained where we'd be going: from Orroroo in the Flinders Ranges, east towards Yunta, north to Koonamore and then south-west along Pipeline Road.

'It's a triangle, Bob. We're doing a triangle.'

I asked how far we'd be riding all up. There was a moment's silence.

'We're not riding, mate. They're wagon camels.'

We would be walking, said my dad. Next to the camels, and for 25 kilometres a day. He paused.

'You have been training, haven't you?'

I said yes, in the sense that I'd managed to keep my legs in pretty much mint/unused condition. I started to panic.

'I thought I was supposed to be practising sitting down.'

My dad's cousin Robyn had married a bushman called Don, and together they raced camels and went on wagon expeditions. This was the first time they were bringing other people along. There would be between nine and fourteen people on the trek. Being in such close quarters with strangers for ten days was not my dad's idea of a good time. He would have preferred to be at home with a book or tinkering in his shed. But his own dad had a reputation for disappearing out the back door every time someone showed up at the front door, and *my* dad was forever trying not to be that guy.

The night before we left Adelaide he did that thing parents do when they're nervous, where they start fussing over their kids instead. He looked at me gruffly and said, 'Now listen, Bob. What are you going to do out there for entertainment?'

'I dunno. I brought a few books.'

'You understand that these are country folk we'll be travelling with. They like different things to us.'

'Well, what about you? What are you going to do?'

'I'm going to look at the fire,' he said. 'Don't worry about me.'

My parents and I drove north from Adelaide to meet up with the crew in Orroroo. On the way we picked up a thirty-one-year-old cameleer called Brian. He had a huge camel-coloured beard and a smile that took over his whole face. 'G'day folks,' he said as he climbed in.

We drove for four hours through small towns and low ranges, alongside dry creek beds and stubbly wheatfields. We peppered Brian with questions about camels ('Is it true that they spit?', 'Can Jewish people eat them?', 'Why don't you ride horses instead?'). He had two camels of his own, Firestorm and Vicky, and every time he talked about them he got a faraway look in his eyes.

In the late afternoon we drove down a dirt driveway and pulled up outside a big shearing shed. The head of our expedition, old bushman Don, came up to the car. From where I was sitting in the back seat, I could only make out his waistline. His jeans were filthy with dirt and about six sizes too big. They were held up by a rope, a belt and a pair of braces.

He leaned in through the window and said, 'Now, the important thing about this trip is not to panic.'

The first thing we were supposed to not panic about was the state of one of the wagons. It had been refurbished by Greg, a local naturalist and council worker who would be joining us on the trek. 'You can tell he worked on the highways,' said Don, pointing at the wagon. 'It's all held together by street signs.'

That wasn't the problem so much as its rickety, lop-sided canopy. The wagon looked as though it wanted to veer off into the bushes and lie down.

I walked over to the holding pen to see if maybe I had a magic touch with camels. This is the persistent dream of dilettantes: that we will, at some point, uncover a superpower that will make sense of lives filled with false starts, failures and endless dabbling.

I stood up on the railing and said, 'Hello, ladies!' to what I would later learn was mostly a bunch of bull-ocks. The camels looked at me with long-lashed eyes. The biggest camel, Weet-Bix, came over and nuz-zled my hand. I stroked his fleshy lips and hummed a Middle Eastern tune I knew; he bit me affectionately on the arm. Things were looking good!

On the morning of departure I asked Brian if he wanted some help wrangling the camels. 'I've got kind of a special rapport with them,' I said, and explained about the deep looks, the nibbling and so forth.

'They've been *biting* you? Mate, you can't let them *do* that!'

So I went and helped my dad instead. He had designed and built a solar-powered electrical system – to power the fridge, freezer and satellite phone – and was ready to install it on the roof of the wagon. I wanted to be useful, so I kept suggesting we bolt things to hard-to-reach poles that only I could climb up to.

Our procession was two wagons long. The main one had a canvas roof and was fitted out with bench seats from an old Kingswood. The smaller wagon was looking pretty rickety, but they'd braced it as best they could.

We spent the rest of the morning loading the main wagon with our worldly possessions, and then (it sounds crazy when you see it written down) attached the wagon to four camels. Those outback camel trains look so stately and peaceful in the photographs! But when our camels felt the weight of the wagon, they bolted and took the wagon bouncing through bushes and rabbit holes. One of the camels started bucking wildly, throwing his head around and generally not taking very good care of our things. Brian was pumping the handbrake and hanging on.

'Pull 'em up, Brian!'

'I'm fucking trying!'

In the ruckus, another four camels broke loose and charged off in the direction of Brian and the wagon. They were tied together but going at high speed.

Brian had, by now, managed to stop the wagon/get tangled in a fence line, but the four-pack of rogue camels headed straight for him.

Don yelled out to me, 'Get between them and the wagon, Bob! Head 'em off!'

Leadership is a hard-to-pin-down quality. But if, after two days of knowing someone, they tell you to jump in front of a pack of charging camels and you find yourself willingly obliging, then they've probably got it.

The camels were looking like a pretty dumb idea, but we were on to a good thing with Don.

We managed to round up the camels and get the wagons back on track. Don took his hat off and wiped the sweat from his face. 'That's normal,' he said. 'They always start off like that. Let's push on.'

One of the reasons people go bush is to trade our old, boring problems (scrounging for rent money, beating the traffic) for new and refreshing ones. On our daily treks we had to pull down stock fences, navigate creek crossings and get cooking fires started in the rain. *This is living!* I thought to myself. My dad didn't quite share my enthusiasm. He was up to his neck in living already. What he really wanted was a nice sit-down.

Getting the camels mustered every morning was a real snafu. There was one problem camel called Blister who'd been raised as a pet and suffered all the same problems as a trust-fund kid. Don was trying to break him in as a wagon camel and get some herd mentality back into him. One morning Blister was really making him sweat. Don was yelling, 'Fucking *boosh down*, you bird-brained bastard!' and the camel – stubborn, indignant – was bellowing back. Meanwhile, Brian and his friend Chantelle (a dreadlocked camel racer) were trying to corral the two lead camels, who'd gotten tangled up somehow.

My dad saw me writing in my diary and came over. He stood next to me for a while. Just the two of us.

'If *I* was writing a book,' he said, 'I'd call it *Why We Invented the Internal Combustion Engine.*'

Brian or Nat usually drove the main wagon. Nat was a bosomy powerhouse who raised a family, kept a menagerie of pets and broke in camels for a living. She wore the same singlet, shorts and thongs the whole trip. Even on frosty nights. One evening she reached into her bra looking for a cigarette, and I saw her pull out a lighter, a tobacco pouch, a packet of tissues, a hunting knife, $20 (*in change*) and a bundle of keys before she looked up and said, 'Oh, here it is. It's in my fucking mouth.' On the fourth day she got kicked full in the face by a camel and started kicking it back.

The smaller wagon was driven by the camp cook, who drank white wine and soda with one hand and swished the reins around with the other. She shouted so relentlessly at her camels (Chrystal and Sapphire) that they could no longer tell what was a command and what was general chitchat. So they ignored her completely and ambled along cheerfully at their own pace. If you wanted to be sure the camels would do something, you had to put on a high-pitched voice or a foreign accent to get their attention.

Don was in charge of getting us out of trouble. ('If Plan A doesn't work, there's always Plan B, and if that doesn't work, well, there's plenty of letters in the alphabet.')

The walkers usually went up ahead or drifted along between the two wagons. We passed through mallee country, sheep stations, along ancient valleys and across plateaus covered in saltbush. If you got far enough ahead there was a strange buzzing stillness. When it was overcast you didn't even hear bird calls. Just the gentle clanking of the approaching wagons, and the muffled shouts, like a distant football game, of people urging the camels up a hill or over boggy ground.

We'd stop once for morning tea, once for lunch, and whenever something went wrong. It never felt like we were covering any great distances, but the nubs of old mountains would appear in the morning and disappear behind us by the end of the day. Greg, a birdwatcher, would come up to us in camp and say, 'Twenty-seven kilometres today, as the crow flies.'

When I got fed up with walking, or with being awake, I would climb into the back of the main wagon, curl up between rifles and saddlebags, and go to sleep. The wagon rocked back and forth, and I dreamed endlessly about women. Of soft voices and deep looks. I dreamed of the brownest eyes I've ever seen, of guitar players kissing me behind stage curtains, of poets reading in small, smoke-filled rooms and looking up coyly between stanzas. I dreamed of warm bodies tangling up in soft sheets, of curved shoulders and tender knees. The relentless masculinity of the bush was starting to wear me down.

In the afternoons we'd pull up an hour or two before sunset and let the camels out to feed. They'd trundle off and start pulling apart the native vegetation, and we would start a fire and get cooking. The camels didn't need to drink once for the entire trip, though I can't say the same for their handlers. They started drinking port from a goon sack at lunch and were pretty much trolleyed by the time dinner was served. Sometimes around the campfire we heard bush stories: about desert crossings, about a guy who had to shoot the bull camel he was riding in the head because he couldn't get it to slow down. But mostly we got the Nat and Chantelle show. They had shouting matches about semen swallowing. (I remember this particularly well because it was the same high-volume argument, almost verbatim, three nights in a row: Chantelle was for, Nat was against. It was Chantelle who kept bringing it up.)

My mum loved it. She thought they were hilarious. But it was all too much for my dad. One morning he said to me, 'That Chantelle's got a mouth like a *sewer.*' Which was a bit rich coming from a guy who, reminiscing about the night of my brother's conception, once said, 'Yep, we should have settled for hand jobs *that* night.' But I got his point, which was that he really wanted to be alone for a while and there was nowhere to sit.

It was a gruelling regime for my parents. They were hardly sleeping at night and were walking all day. When the wagons stopped for lunch, the came-leers would climb down to stretch their legs, and my parents would look around desperately for some-where to rest. My dad didn't want to sit on the ground, because he feared he wouldn't be able to get back up. I started climbing onto the wagon at lunchtime and pulling down camp stools.

On the fifth day, I was walking with my dad, and he said that he wanted to go home early. I was shocked. I don't think I've ever seen my dad give up.

'What does Mum think?'

He grunted. 'She won't even talk about it.'

He was looking pretty beaten. He'd walked 30 kilometres that day and was chilled to the bone. (For days after the trip, he would walk around our house shivering and trying to get warm. 'It's *cold*,' he kept saying, when it wasn't.) He'd developed cracked lips, a patchy white beard and various other ailments that had afflicted the early white explorers. My mum wasn't looking crash hot either. Her face was red and puffy because, for complicated reasons, she didn't believe in sunscreen.

There's a peculiar anguish to seeing your own par-ents suffer. If it's your children suffering, you know or hope that it's because they're still building their characters, that the world will accommodate them somehow. But if it's your parents, you know that things are probably only going to get harder for them. The world for them is a cruise liner steaming towards the horizon, leaving them bobbing alone in the vast, lonely ocean with only each other.

My dad said, 'Jesus Christ, Bob, do you have to say this shit out loud? It's pretty bleak.'

We trudged through flat, heavily grazed country that had the feeling of a ghost town. Rain had washed out some tracks ahead, so when we reached the ruins of the Waukaringa pub we turned around and started back the way we came.

The camels never trudged. They held their heads up high, like queens at a ball, for days. A horse pulls in a straight line. But the camels were always looking around as they walked, with a prospective optimism that eluded us now that we were heading back the way we came.

I tried to entertain my dad with half-baked theories about possessions. I had visited a camping store on the day before the trip, and everything in there had felt so *essential*. I got so excited by the gadgetry that I would have blown all my money in one go if I'd had any. And what you realise, once you actually leave the city, is that it's all crap. That's why they never have those stores out in the country. I can't think of one thing in those shops that we could have used out there. What we needed was a pair of pliers and some wire. Throughout the journey we fixed everything with that combination. The broken steering column, the billy can, the bracket on the solar-powered system. I remember being impressed by the quality of Don's camp oven. It was a thing that would last a lifetime. I'm through with flim-flam, I said. What is it about city living? All I want to do when I'm there is *buy* stuff. What I want is just a few beautiful, useful things.

My dad asked, 'Is that why you bought that camel skin?'

Well, okay. So you can get fooled in reverse too. At the campfire one night I was talking to the manager of the local meatworks and got a great price on a camel skin. Twenty-five bucks! Say what you want about my decision-making, but don't tell me that's not a bargain. When I arranged to buy it, I thought, *This will become one of my most useful possessions.*

I've been back home for two months now, and I'm lumbered with this camel skin. I find myself in the ridiculous situation of trying to find an apartment big enough to keep it in. Too many people have gone to too much trouble for me to throw it away. Robyn drove it from the Flinders Ranges to Adelaide. My parents – who did finish the trek, and walked the whole way – salted it themselves and sent it to a tannery. Now I have it rolled up in the corner of my room. Just as I have the image of my dad and mum on the last day of the trip, utterly miserable, but walking side by side and leaning into each other on the road to Orroroo.

# 5

# How to Make It in Business

The idea for the magazine came when I was still living on Sydney Road, Brunswick, with Manoli and our American friend, Andy. The flat was above a music shop and across the road from our favourite bookstore (as well as a now-defunct Afghan restaurant called The Lazy Camel). Trams clattered past our windows in the daytime, and at night-time a parade of drunks stomped by on the way from one pub, which closed at three, to another one down the road, which was open till four.

'It's like a zombie march,' said Andy disgustedly.

We held them in the greatest contempt, except on the nights when we were down there with them.

The flat had five bedrooms, each with its own

bathroom, and was rumoured to be an ex-brothel. Also living with us were Laura (a musician) and Bisi (an illustrator.) We were all from interstate or over-seas. The same was true, at least in the beginning, of everyone working on the magazine. We had come from small towns and unfashionable cities, and now we were living in the middle of everything, filled with Big City dreams.

For four years we ran what was Australia's greatest (and admittedly only) short-story magazine. We washed dishes to pay writers and plundered stationery from universities where our siblings had access to office supplies. Everyone knows that magazines don't make money in the beginning, but we were surprised to find it didn't make money in the middle or the end either.

When sales of the first issue started coming in, Andy mentioned that he might like to spend his share of the proceeds on a snorkelling holiday to the Great Barrier Reef. I was all for it until someone asked, 'Don't we need the money from the first issue to pay for the second one?'

'Oh God,' I said, 'it's a Ponzi scheme.'

In the beginning, we couldn't afford an office, so we rented the corridor leading to someone else's.

Most of it was taken up by a large immovable work-bench that was impossible to sit at.

'It's more of a standing desk,' said the guy renting it to us.

Harriet joined the magazine when it was still in its corridor phase. Andy and I had tried to solve the problem of the immovable workbench by arranging our furniture on top of it.

'I like it,' she said. 'Two storeys!'

Other people joined the magazine and brought with them talent, energy and ideas. It was our copy-editor Kate's idea to check the magazine for mistakes before sending it to the printer.

'Maybe we could do this every time,' I said.

For a while, we, or really I, experimented with interns. After our first issue, Andy returned to America and everyone else went away on holiday. The office was getting lonely. I began hiring as interns anyone who expressed an interest in the magazine and several who didn't. Soon we had six interns and only five chairs, and it was a constant battle to keep people busy enough that they wouldn't notice. In something of a role reversal, I couldn't stop offering to make every-one coffee, so I was alone anyway, but in the kitchen, and it was only once everyone had gone home that

I was able to get any work done.

When Harriet came back, she took a look around and said, 'Maybe we should be hiring interns on more of a one-at-a-time basis from now on.'

One of our finest inventions was a fake accountant called Linda McMackerson. Bookstores were often tardy with their payments, but we loved them and wanted to remain on friendly terms. If a bookstore was late with a payment, it was Linda who sent them a series of stern and increasingly disturbing emails. We tried to create an aura of fear around her. We spread rumours that she was an Olympic silver medallist in the javelin. And that she was still angry about coming second. And that she still had her javelin. Nevertheless, our greatest financial achievement in that first year was being paid $30 by our landlord for catching the office mouse.

*

Chloe, one of our editors, said that the closest she's come to the experience of putting out an issue of the magazine – in the degree of stress and logistical mayhem – was being evicted from her house. We were trying to put out four issues a year.

But the magazine was much more impressive than the circumstances it was created in. We published our heroes and sold to bookstores, newsagents and subscribers all over Australia. There is a country town called Taradale in which, according to our sales figures, 5 per cent of the population read *The Canary Press.*

Somehow, without meaning to, and without really knowing that such a thing existed, we became part of the Melbourne Literary Scene. It was like running joyously along a beach and accidentally joining up with a triathlon. Suddenly you find yourself jostling for space, measuring your progress not against the beach but against the people around you.

On our camel trip I had overheard two cameleers talking. Brian said, 'The New South Wales camel scene could be so much fun ... if only it wasn't so *bitchy.*' And I thought, *Egad! Even in the camel world!*

\*

I struggled with our technocratic age. I had never had an office job; I'd barely worked indoors before. People were always recommending fancy software that would make our lives easier. You'd go to install it and then find out you were missing some sort of plug-in, so you'd download that and it would say you needed to install a new operating system first and would you like to back everything up? But you didn't have the hard drive, and pretty soon you'd be standing in the long, lonely aisles of Officeworks again, when all you'd wanted to do was schedule a lunch.

One night, trying to meet a print deadline, I was up late, making last-minute typesetting changes. In InDesign, there is a shortcut – 'shift + W' – for toggling between full-screen and normal view. I was toggling away, and it was only when we got three thousand copies of the magazine back from the printers that I realised I had littered the text with capital Ws.

I lunged into the office with a dozen bottles of white-out, and said, 'We can fix this.'

Beth, our assistant publisher, put her foot down. 'The only thing worse,' said Beth, 'than receiving a magazine filled with Ws is getting one where some clown has tried to cover them up with liquid paper.'

In the most shameful episode of my literary life, I discovered that I had somehow deleted two paragraphs of a story by the late, great J.G. Ballard and replaced them with one of my heinous Ws.

*

There was always the problem of money. We put huge amounts of energy into applying for grants. The problem with grants, apart from not getting them, is that after writing an application you no longer want to make art or magazines or love or babies ever again.

We attempted all sorts of things to keep the magazine running. Bede suggested buying mice at wholesale price, releasing them in the office and then recapturing them at $30 a pop. But with our landlord away on holidays they would have just been more mouths to feed.

Running a magazine (or any other business) with so few resources is like driving a car with its suspension shot: you feel every bump. When it got too much, I lay in my swag at night and wrote resignation letters, but I never knew who to send them to. I sent one to my mum, who said she liked the characters but didn't understand the ending.

*

We began striving for new heights of professionalism. I'd even started living in a house.

One night, working late, I found some photocopied pages from a management guide. It was written in the collective first person from the point of view of the staff.

'We are pack animals,' it said. 'Treating us as your friend is not always an act of kindness. We need to know our place in order to thrive and be happy.' I was thumping the table and saying, *Yes! Yes!*, until I turned the page and realised I was reading from Chloe's dog-training manual.

I told her about it the next day and she said, 'Man, that stuff doesn't even work on dogs.'

The magazine went from saddle-stitched to perfect-bound. We began selling in airports and train stations.

And then we were awarded one of those grants. The grant covered the printing costs for another year, but it did little to improve our circumstances. As we laboured on, we realised that it had cunningly locked us into making at least three more issues. Previously, we had been working for literary glory, for the short story, for the idea that we might help expand our country's sense of itself, for each other. And with the persistent dream that we might one day generate for ourselves a modest income. But a creeping shift had taken place: it had begun to feel as though we were unpaid employees of the Literary Industrial Complex.

People wrote emails thanking us for 'providing a home for writers'.

'We're not an orphanage,' said Bede. 'We're doing it because we *believe* in something.'

We were frequently asked to provide mission statements – for panels and grant applications – and they were becoming harder and harder to write. I was constantly on the phone to our general manager, Susie, asking: *'What* is it we believe in, again?'

As we approached our tenth issue, we began running out of steam. Normally we would all go home for the summer holidays and come back refreshed and rejuvenated. But when I arrived back in Melbourne, the well had failed to fill up again.

*

For a long time, I couldn't work out if the magazine was a success or a failure. Couldn't work out if our ten issues were like flowers that had bloomed briefly in the desert, or corpses littering the road of literary ambition.

Years later, I was invited by one of our prestigious universities to give a talk called *How to Make It in Business*, and I stood in the foyer beforehand staring hungrily at everyone's muffins. I was one of three speakers. We were speaking to an auditorium of about a hundred high-school graduates, all of them prospective arts students, and we were meant to persuade them to take up an education in the arts. I did some rough calculations. If we succeeded in convincing all of them, then Melbourne University stood to make about $4 million in revenue. We, the speakers, weren't being paid anything. It was a Ponzi scheme alright, but we weren't at the top.

I stood up and told the students more or less what I have told you, thinking it my duty to warn them off. I tried to remain gruff and world-weary, but halfway through the speech I found myself getting overexcited, buoyed by the sight of all those young, eager faces. Forgive me: I found I had no desire to warn them off at all. I hoped, instead, that they would leap boldly off cliffs and, as Kurt Vonnegut once said, grow wings on the way down.

# 6

# The Stopover

My trip overseas had been a failure, and not even a spectacular one. I'd gone away only with the vague plan of coming home feeling better. I sat alone in romantic villas reading books by the dim glow of the mood lighting, bobbed around in tropical oceans, and never really worked out what I was supposed to be doing there.

My hope for redemption lay on my way home, in that great tourist mecca: Singapore Airport. I had twelve hours between flights, and though I had fluffed the trip I was determined to ace the stopover.

In an airport you can be anyone: no one knows your story; they only know you're going somewhere. At 8.55 a.m. I strode into the terminal with the feeling

I had my whole life ahead of me, probably because I hadn't done anything with it yet.

A woman in uniform said, 'Transiting, sir?'

I doffed my hat and said, 'Thank you, madam,' without breaking stride.

Inside, people bustled around on jazzy carpets, pianos tinkled in the background, and tropical plants had the time of their lives in the rich potted soils of the atrium. For the next two hours I lived like a rich man: I strolled through the butterfly gardens, drank mocktails by the rooftop pool and lounged in massage chairs, watching everyone else rush for their flights. When I ran out of things to do, I just powerwalked indiscriminately through the airport. If you want to look accomplished, that's how you do it.

Whenever I'm around duty-free shops, I start to believe strongly that I have more money than I really do. Woozy from all the perfume, I imagine myself to be some sort of high-flyer, the sort of person who can afford $300 bags, based mainly on the irrefutable evidence that I'm standing in a shop with $300 bags in it.

Worse is when I get the idea that by shopping duty-free I'm somehow rorting the system, that with a few cunning purchases I could restore my fortunes.

I could buy all the things that rich people buy, *but at duty-free prices*, while everyone else (those fools!) is stuck paying full price. Usually, only the imminent departure of my flight can save me from myself. But that was still hours away, which is how I came to be buying discounted bottles of chartreuse with my credit card.

It was thrilling! Waving my credit card around and speaking in a manlier voice than usual. But the thrill wore off like drugs, and as I stood in the thoroughfare holding all the chartreuse, I began to wonder if the main business of flying was really shopping; if the bag checks, the security, the wand-waving were just sneaky ways of making us feel like members of some high society – more distinguished than the bums outside.

However, there was important work to do. I had been travelling for three weeks and had failed to have any of the meaningful revelations that travel is famous for, so I was hoping to knock together a few thoughts on the way home.

At 11.45 a.m. I took a seat by the windows and sat for the longest time reflecting on my trip, until, at 11.52, I looked up and was horrified to see how little time had passed. The minutes creaked by. I tried reading from a beautiful novel, but it was like a voice coming from far away. The book was a lyrical exploration of the human spirit, and even though I'd been away for three weeks, I obviously hadn't self-improved enough to appreciate its subtle charms. I kept wandering over to the shelves filled with airport novels, craving some action. There were only nine hours until my flight home and I was still the same person as before.

*

On the tarmac, nothing much was happening except the quiet miracle of flight. I was itching for someone to talk to. People rarely mention how claustrophobic travelling is. You can go to the furthest-flung lands, but you can't escape your own banal interior mono-logue. (*That jungle's the same colour as the carpet in my office! This taxi smells like grandma!*) I went over to the luggage store and asked the saleswoman to tell me about Samsonite again, but her heart wasn't in it. People were leaving the country rather than talk to me, and it was refilling at the same rate with new people who didn't want to talk to me either. In the absence of anything better to do, and because it was almost lunchtime, I toddled over to one of the bars.

The only possibly meaningful thing that had happened on my trip was that I had seen a manta ray. She had glided past with such majesty that I was sure it meant something. That day in the water, I bobbed hopefully nearby, but whatever message she was sending kept getting distorted by the choppy waves and the other snorkellers, jostling for a photo. Close up she looked harried, as though she had once been the guardian of an ancient secret but now she was just trying to get by.

Everyone else comes home with photos of themselves sitting on beaches, atop mountains or posing with local orphans (never the miserable one). But most of travel is waiting: sitting for hours at the wrong bus stop, or lying around in cheap hotels trying not to masturbate because you're supposed to be seeing some temples later. Or, like me in the airport bar, practising the fine art of being bored. I texted my religious brother back home:

'Is this what being a Christian is like? Just sitting around waiting for your plane to come?'

He wrote back: 'Hey mate, pretty busy right now, let's talk later. We don't just sit around, you know ...'

I sat there and thought about that.

The best photographic record of my travels was

taken in New Zealand, in the days of film cameras. I came home drunk one night to my dark tent and went through a whole roll of film using flash photography to try to find my torch. Travel? There it is.

*

At 2 p.m. I tried a different bar. You can do that in Singapore Airport. I went up to the rooftop and moped around in the cactus garden while the sun burned through the clouds. I hate afternoons. The way they lie there in wait, lurking like a midlife crisis. I can't think of a single good thing that's happened between the hours of 2 and 4 p.m. The cactus garden served beer at least, so I put down my bag, my book and the chartreuse, and ordered one. I sipped on my beer, poked a few cacti. One of the spines stuck right in my finger, which is exactly what you'd expect from an afternoon.

At 3.30 p.m. my flight felt further away than it had at 8.55 a.m.

At 3.45 I wondered if I would find God.

Then, at 4 p.m., the sun dipped below the skyline of cacti, and the afternoon – that horror show – was over. Time seemed to find its rhythm again, and the next few hours skipped along. At 8.20 p.m., finally, for the first time on my trip, something happened: my plane started taxiing off without me.

As to my actual departure time, it's clear I'd been going more by vibe than, say, what was written on the ticket. It seemed an oversight, not to have spent more of the intervening hours studying my boarding pass. When my flight was in the final stages of boarding, I was in one of the massage chairs, reading a self-help book about failure, and having the time of my life.

My leisurely twelve-hour stopover culminated in me making a desperate sprint for the boarding gate and running into a glass door. The Jetstar employee had some sympathy, but mostly for the door.

'Is that my plane?' I asked, clutching my nose and pointing into the now-dark night.

'That *was* your plane, sir.'

I sprinted over to the transfer desk, thinking frantically about all the things I could have done differently. I yelled, 'Stop the plane!'

'Name, please,' said the woman at the desk.

'Robert Skinner,' I panted. 'With a "J". In the middle, I mean. That's my middle name. Well, not "J", obviously. Joseph. Listen, I'm supposed to be on that flight.'

'Sir, that flight is gone,' she said.

And it was true. I could no longer tell what I was pointing at. I sagged like a tent.

She punched a few buttons, made a call and then said: 'We're sending someone over.'

'To put me on another flight?' I asked hopefully.

'To escort you out of the airport, sir. Only passengers with valid tickets are allowed inside the transit area.'

A young gentleman from the airline came over to walk me out.

As I was gathering my things, he spotted the chartreuse.

'Sir, you're going to have to return those bottles.'

He led me through the shop, and I followed sheepishly, like a shoplifting child. An older woman at the checkout looked from me to the bottles.

'You no want?'

'Can't have,' I said.

The Jetstar steward led me towards immigration, and he made some calls as we whooshed along.

'So, we have no more flights leaving tonight?' he said on his phone. 'What about tomorrow morning? ... Oh ... Wednesday? ... Thursday?'

Then he listed off some other days of the week.

After three weeks drifting aimlessly through Indonesia, and so close to home, disaster had struck. It felt great. Say what you will about rock bottom, but at least it's sturdy.

At immigration, under 'primary reason for visiting Singapore', I wrote, 'Idiot.' And as they led me through immigration, I was grinning like one too.

# PART TWO

# 7

# Kings of Sweden

**M**uch to my annoyance, Melbourne kept getting voted the 'World's Most Liveable City', which, if things aren't going well for you, makes you feel the opposite of Frank Sinatra in 'New York, New York': If I can't make it here, where *can* I make it?

Our lives were filled with such rigmarole it was amazing we had time for jobs. In supermarkets, they'd started making us check out our own groceries. But was there a corresponding price decrease? Was there fuck.

A significant part of living in Melbourne is planning to leave it. At parties, people wax lyrical about moving to the country. 'Except,' the Melburnians continue, 'I just couldn't live without the theatre, live music,' etc., and they list the things they've been to that year – all of which an out-of-towner would manage in one leisurely weekend.

I tried to escape more than most. (Or, I tried the normal amount, and complained more than most.) But Melbourne has its tricks. It has a way of impressing its importance upon you. Even getting away for a weekend seems impossible. You're just so *busy*. But if you do manage to get out – if, say, a friend kidnaps you in the middle of the night and bundles you into the back of a car with a sleeping bag – you will find yourself standing in a paddock under a tree, with clear horizons in every direction, telling anyone within earshot: 'I had absolutely nothing on.'

*

I was invited to MC a wedding in Sweden. From Stockholm, I travelled north with my fellow MC, a Swedish sculptor called Jenny. We drove through fields and forests, and past farmhouses that were all painted the same shade of red because, she told me, after one of the wars it was the only colour going around. We drove for two days until we arrived in

Vindeln, a small town up near the Arctic Circle, on the banks of a wild river.

Friends came from all over and were billeted to homes in the village. Our days were filled with swimming, sex, the possibility of moose. You couldn't put a foot down in the forest without stepping on some berry or other. I felt like a miner who, having been trapped underground, had finally emerged into sunshine, green grass and the arms of loved ones. We ate wild boar, set up for the wedding and lazed by the river. The idea of going home was preposterous – like being ordered back underground to fetch the company toolbox.

On the evening before the wedding, Jenny told the story of a Swedish king who had tried and failed to train an army of moose. It was a rabble, she said. The moose were foragers, for one thing – you couldn't feed them on hay alone, like you can with horses – so they were always wandering off, looking for something better to eat. And as soon as they heard the sound of battle they couldn't be coaxed onwards for love or money. In her telling of it, this all happened in the winter, when the moose had shed their antlers. So that on the day of the battle – when the rugged-up king turned to his general, with dawning comprehension, and said, 'These animals aren't listening to us at *all*' – the fields were full of moose romping about like bald babies in the snow.

The wedding was a success. Rowan and Ronja looked beautiful in their traditional Swedish dress. We wrote and performed a play in their honour. People gave speeches. Only minor injuries were sustained during the tug of war. In a pergola surrounded by forest, we ate, drank and danced as the Arctic sun ambled through the trees at knee height.

Towards the drunker end of the evening, when the party had moved into the 'disco barn', and everything was being lost in the haze from the smoke machine, I remember holding people's faces in my hands and saying, 'We can't go back. Don't you understand? We are the moose. The moose is us. *The moose is us.*' Until it was time to go home.

# 8

# House Party

The pandemic arrived in Australia at the same time I did. (A coincidence, probably.)

I had been staying in Vietnam as part of an elaborate plan to save on rent. Like many of my money-saving schemes, it had turned out to be considerably more expensive than the normal way of doing things. I arrived at Southern Cross Station, broke, just as everyone else was making for cover. I, too, wanted to go under house arrest, but in which house?

I stayed for a few nights on my friend Amanda's blow-up mattress, then for a week in another friend's temporarily vacated apartment, until I got a gig house-sitting a mansion in North Melbourne.

The house was on a wide and peaceful street with eucalyptus trees running down its middle. They performed a magical trick of the light: they softened and filtered it when it was too harsh and seemed to scatter it generously when it was in short supply. Had such things been allowed, each tree could have hosted its own picnic.

I entered through a heavy wooden door and carried my box of personal effects down the hallway – past the study, the master bedroom, the twin-share, the second bathroom, the atrium, the dining hall, the grand piano, the sitting room – and into the kitchen, where I spent three days looking for the fridge. (I have form: I once had a job interview that was going great until I stood up to leave and couldn't find my way out of the room.)

I was sleeping in the certificate room – a study-cum-spare-bedroom upon whose walls hung the many diplomas, degrees and PhDs of the owners' high-achieving daughters. Every morning I awoke surrounded by accolades.

In a burst of civic enthusiasm, I applied for a job driving deliveries for Australia Post. Because everyone was in isolation, I had to interview myself on video. I set up in front of the bay windows and described at length my love of parcels, post and driving trucks. My application was rejected in the first round. Outside, the streets had emptied, the traffic had disappeared, but some things hadn't changed: the world was still full of jobs you didn't really want and couldn't even get.

I wandered out onto the verandah. The last of the day's sun was hitting the top of a eucalypt across the road while a squabbling flock of lorikeets settled into its branches. A nurse walked past on her way home from a nearby hospital. I tried to lead everyone in a standing ovation, like they did in Britain, but there was no one else around and it came off more condescending than I would have liked.

The next morning I put myself in charge of poems. I dragged my wireless printer from the boot of my car and set it up in the study, where it continued its decade-long refusal to live up to its name. But after a day or two of wrestling I got it going, more or less. I began mailing out curated bundles of poems to my friends, so they would have a poem to read for every day of the pandemic. The study was filled with dog-eared anthologies, stamps, envelopes and the smell of my protesting printer. For two weeks I was able to maintain the atmosphere of an (understaffed) newsroom during wartime. But I ran out of steam well before the pandemic did.

There loomed ever larger the problem of my heart. Twice in the past three years (once, recently) it had been poleaxed by love. I was trying to think of this as a good thing: if you're run over by two trucks in a row at least you can say, *Well, I've found the highway.*

But there was a rising hysteria to my self-consolations. I paced from room to room like the Beast in *Beauty and the Beast*, took distraught saunas and bought something called anti-aging cream after becoming convinced that I was doing permanent damage to my face by looking crestfallen all the time.

The worst thing was that there was nowhere to go. You could only stand there and let it crash over you.

In the mansion, the weeks, and then the months, dragged by until – like windows thrown open in a stuffy room – friends were allowed back into our lives. In ones and twos, then in threes and fours, they came to the mansion, and I cooked them dinner or drank with them by a fireplace. It was one of these friends who told me that, technically, it wasn't a mansion but merely a 'large Edwardian home'. Well, maybe. But he hadn't been the one tasked with trying to fill it. And he yelled all this from the kitchen as Caitlin, Annie and I were giggling and skipping across the tiles from the sauna to the swimming pool, and Bill was off taking a work call in another wing of the house, so ... make of that what you will.

*

After the first lockdown was lifted (and before Melbourne went into its second, third, fourth, fifth and sixth lockdowns) I got a job working at my favourite bookshop. The shop was directly across the road from the flat that Manoli, Andy and I had shared when I had first moved to Melbourne. Whether I had come full circle – or whether, in the great journey of life, I had succeeded merely in crossing the road – was not yet known.

The shop had been run by the same couple for thirteen years. They and the bookhop's full-timer, Megan, each had their own distinct set of regulars. You could usually guess to whom these customers belonged as soon as they arrived at the door, and they were always disappointed and appalled to find some other staff member at the counter.

But it was wonderful being in that thicket of books and people. The days would begin in quiet communion, with the books breathing softly on the shelves. Then you would open the door and put the sign out on the footpath. Customers would drift in, and by lunchtime the shop would be filled with people.

The beginnings of a job, like the beginnings of love, are filled with a renewed attention. It is as though you are learning new things about the world every day. But it almost never lasts. After a while, you start trudging through days like cattle. In the bookshop, it wasn't time that stripped the sheen from the job, but another set of restrictions. This time there was an 8 p.m. curfew, you had to wear a mask outside even if you were standing alone in the middle of a paddock, and for the first time in my life I needed a permission slip to travel to work. (I'd only ever used them for getting *out* of work.)

*So ... this is growing up*, I thought. Well, I didn't like it.

My friend James was approaching the second lockdown with either more or less maturity; I couldn't tell. 'Love the masks,' he said on the phone. 'Love the curfew, love all that … spices things up a bit.'

My living situation was much cosier this time around. I had moved into a Thornbury share house with one fireplace instead of five, and I was living not alone but with two housemates and a farting staffy. I also had what we hoped would be classified by the government as an 'intimate partner'. The rules were unclear. To be safe, we recorded an hour-long sex tape and carried it with us at all times, in case we were stopped on the way to each other's home.

The only cop who was willing to watch it looked up in disgust partway through: 'This is just a video of you two eating mushrooms and talking about cricket. I thought you said it was a sex tape?'

'When you're in love, dear fellow, every tape is a sex tape.'

*

In the bookshop we began to realise what an enjoyable business model it had been letting customers come in and find their own books. The restrictions turned us into warehouse workers. Inside the shop, we would pick, pack, label and process online orders while the owners drove around delivering them to people's doors. Customers were ordering books that no one had seen in real life since 2017. Meanwhile, the phone rang off the hook. I took so many phone orders that I began to recognise patterns in credit card numbers and was able to guess some people's digits in advance. Customers found this less endearing than you might think.

People were finding everything less endearing. On the phone, they had gone from exclaiming, 'You're delivering? For *free*? Wow, gosh, thank you!' to saying, 'Well, I need it by lunchtime today or you might as well burn it.'

Parents were increasingly unable to deal with the news that we had, yet again, sold out of *Poo Bingo*. I heard the owner losing it on the phone too: 'Whattya mean, books about eggs?'

Just as the bookshop had been reduced to its crudest function and stripped of everything that had made it enjoyable (the customers, the bustle, the larking about), so, too, had our lives been stripped of lateral possibility. You could still walk to work, and return home afterwards, but there was no prospect of being waylaid en route. The greatest thrill available to most of us was putting the bins out fifteen minutes after curfew.

You began to notice that the things deemed 'essential services' were not the things essential to people's lives but to the running of the city. Music was out; construction was in.

The city had been deprived of everything that might make living there worthwhile – the friends, the bars, the chance encounters, the beautiful strangers, the music, the arts, the community sports ... and we were left only with the price of admission.

I began walking to work along the Merri Creek. It's true that we were allowed an hour of daily exercise, but the arbitrary, mandated nature of it made it impossible to enjoy. On my creek walks I was at least *going* somewhere ... In the mornings, the air was cold and crisp. The wattles were in full bloom.

If you want to know what middle age feels like, you can stand on a footbridge over a creek. Facing upstream, the creek rushes towards you, swollen and burbling, bursting its banks. Middle age is the moment on the bridge when you turn to the rail on the other side, breathe out and begin to watch it flow away.

Well, I was damned if I was going to fall for that one. If I was ever going to cross over it would be by way of a graceful pirouette not a submission of will.

(That was in the mornings. As I trudged home in the evenings, forget middle age, old age itself could have chased me down on a walker and tackled me to the ground. Sometimes, on the way home, I was so tired that I had to sit and nap on people's fences.)

At night, my legs twitched in my sleep. Before the pandemic, I had played for a mixed-gender pub football team called The Easybeats. My responsibilities had been playing fullback and writing the team newsletter.

Fullback is a position characterised by mounting dread, punctuated with bursts of terror. But the pleasure of spoiling an opponent (rather than taking a mark yourself in the forward line) is like the difference between building a sandcastle and kicking one over.

There is the possibility of grace: with the constant threat of calamity, the bond with your fellow defenders strengthens quickly. (This can develop into something of a martyr complex, which annoys the coaches so much they move you into the forward line.) And from the back line, you can begin a play that unfolds down the length of the field. At times, it was akin to poetry.

Sometimes I'd stand at fullback wondering how one might build a whole life from this – how to be part of a ragtag team working beautifully towards some shared end. And then I'd hear the coach yelling from the edges of my daydream. 'Robert, for fuck's sake, live in the moment!' or something. I'd look up to see the full-forward off on another lead, and I'd be after him.

After the match we would eat and drink together. During lockdowns we missed even that.

So what do you do? Well, if you happen to scoop up the ball in the back lines, you run. And as you stream down the wing, ball in hand, it will feel like no one can catch you, and no one will; and sure, it will turn out later that the siren had gone for half-time and people had started traipsing off the ground already, but still.

# 9

# Car Sick

**W**hen the car was delivered, Melbourne was in lockdown again. Or still. I was busy having another one of the world's most boring dreams. One night I'd dreamed that I was asleep, but in slightly cleaner sheets. (They weren't; I checked.)

The premier, Dan Andrews, had just closed playgrounds across the city, to punish everyone for an engagement party south of the river that had breached health orders. Politically, it was hard to know what to hope for: the state government was all stick and no carrot; the Opposition couldn't even find the donkey. But promises had been made regarding the lifting of lockdown, and I was getting vaccinated twice a week to try to bring the state numbers up.

As soon as the 5-kilometre travel limit was removed I planned to start driving. And when I hit sand (it was a four-wheel drive) I planned to keep going.

That was as far as I'd considered; it was not a time for dreaming big. One night, my housemate Kyrié dreamed that she'd bought a jar of chilli paste for the house. The next morning, she opened the fridge and discovered, with horror, that she had. 'Man, my brain's not even *imagining* things anymore, it's just remembering the highlights from yesterday.'

*

Different cars have different personalities. My friend Bede had a 1992 Toyota Corolla that had been rusting in a corner of his yard for more than a year. When he had to move house, we set aside two days to get it up and running again. To our disappointment, all we had to do was fill the radiator from a garden hose, turn the key, and the car roared back to life. It took off down the laneway, trailing fairy lights. True, it wasn't much of a stopper, but it was a goer. That car might forget your name, might forget everything else, but it would never forget how to drive.

This car was a 2003 Mazda Bravo. When the delivery driver reversed it off the truck, it blew huge clouds of smoke. Even once he was safely out and handing over the keys and paperwork, he kept glancing back at it, as you might in the company of a troublesome horse.

I shook out the mats, then began making small repairs that were in the realm of my mechanical knowledge: fixing the headlights, changing the glow plugs. Mechanical work is such a relief from creative work. At the end of a day, something is either fixed or it's not. You don't stand there looking at a gearbox thinking, *Yes, but is it* me?

I found I could while away hours at some small task, like a man digging his way through a prison wall with a spoon. I spent a whole evening with a torch and a telescopic magnet trying to extricate a bolt from the engine bay. True, it wouldn't have needed doing if I hadn't dropped it down there myself three days earlier, but try telling that to my sense of satisfaction.

*

On a good day, I would describe its colour as bronze. On a bad day, beige. It was not love at first sight, as it had been with Bede's Corolla. More like a wary cohabitation. I couldn't get a proper read on it. It was like a song coming through with too much static. Maybe because I hadn't seen it in its natural habitat – it should have been bouncing along a bush track, not rotting away in lockdown like the rest of us. Maybe also because it still had the previous owner's greasy fingerprints on it. And it had started making clunking noises.

(The car, for its part, had probably felt me fiddling amateurishly with its drive shaft and wasn't sold on me, either.)

Sometimes you're too close to something to properly tell. My friend Alex lived nearby. He sent me an excited text: *Is that your 4WD out the front?!?* Then he sent the photo. It was my housemate Lucas's, a Troop Carrier.

*No mate, mine's the brown one directly behind it.*

One morning, Kyrié and I drove into town for PCR tests. She told me that when she was younger, she had blown a head gasket in her car and had tried to ignore it and keep driving, even as smoke poured from the engine and people (mostly men of a certain age who might have been accused of treating their bodies in the same way) yelled at her to *Pull over! Pull over!*

'Did you make it?'

'Yeah! Well, sort of. I drove it to the dealership and traded it in for a bicycle.'

We made it too. The tests came back negative. We were, it turned out, merely hungover and depressed.

Some people bang on about how lockdowns provide an opportunity for 'reflection'. That may have been true of the first one, but by the time the fifth and sixth lockdowns rolled over us, there was nothing left to reflect *on*. So you would end up deconstructing yourself, or unravelling, and I wasn't about to try that again, so I learnt to deconstruct the car instead.

My repairs became increasingly ambitious, to the point where the car was so often in pieces that I rarely got to drive it. It was my hope that if I changed every part myself, I might finally understand it.

\*

Then suddenly, and somewhat inconveniently, lockdown was lifted. I was expected back in Adelaide.

Removing a drive shaft days before you're due to arrive in Adelaide does not, I admit, sound like the behaviour of someone who really wants to go to Adelaide. But I did want to. (I think.) The closer I got to departure, the more disarray the car and I were in.

It turns out any idiot can take out a drive shaft. The hard part is getting it back in.

A single bolt, like a well-placed bureaucrat, can ruin everything. It was possibly the least consequential bolt in the whole car, but it was stuck and had ground everything to a halt. Like a demented king, I stayed up late obsessing about it and ordering things online, so that the next day the streets were filled with delivery vans racing around the city to bring me various tools pertaining to the removal of this bolt.

By the time I drilled it out (and replaced the u-joints and reinstalled the drive shaft), there was no time to take the car for a proper test drive. I loaded it up and headed for Adelaide.

I have described the Zen-like satisfaction of fixing things: of taking them apart, cleaning the components and laying them carefully aside for future reassembly. But there is also the distinctly un-Zen-like experience of driving in something you have put together yourself. It all makes perfect sense when you're disassembling it. It's only once you're on the main road that you realise you were in no way qualified to put it back together again.

I edged the car up to 60 kilometres an hour, and it still seemed okay. I turned onto the highway and approached 80, clenched against the expectation of a drive shaft spinning out of control and crashing through the underside of the car. I pushed it towards 90 and all of a sudden I could smell something like burning toast. *Oh God, what's wrong now?* But it was just me, having a series of tiny strokes from the stress.

*

People in Melbourne had long since given up on the idea of emerging from lockdowns like a butterfly from a chrysalis. When I was in high school, my friend's mum rescued some battery hens and released them into a huge and beautiful yard. They were so daunted by all that space that they ran straight over to the fence, sat down and stuck their necks through the wire. We were more like those chickens.

When I got to Adelaide, I couldn't think of anything to do other than hang out at my parents' house and take the car apart again, in preparation for the drive back to Melbourne.

This time I had my dad to help. Together, we tried to solve what seemed a simple problem: the 4WD-mode light kept coming on when it shouldn't and turning off when it should. But the deeper we dug, the more baffled we became.

'No wonder you can't discern the car's true spirit,' said my dad. 'It's all ... mucked up inside.'

We began running tests. I crawled around under the car, plugging and unplugging things, while my dad called out the readings from the multimeter.

'You should be writing this down,' he said.

It was pretty basic and easily remembered stuff, but sometimes it's simpler to humour your parents. So we ran tests, and I made a big show of recording the results in a notebook.

The next day, my dad had taken apart the module that controlled the 4WD/2WD system and was testing it on his bench.

'What reading did we get on the indicator switch?' he asked.

Who could possibly know such a thing?

'We tested it yesterday.'

We did? I flicked through my notes. 'Indicator switch ... indicator switch ... ' Aha! 'Yeah – it works.'

'What was the reading?'

'Um ... ' I held the notebook closer. 'It just says "Indicator switch" and then a big tick.'

*

The more I learnt about cars – this one in particular – the more I discovered about the character of the previous owner (or the previous owner's mechanic), and the depths of their nitwittery. Sometimes it bordered on vandalism. Normally, when you look underneath a newly purchased car and find a recently installed part you think, *Great! I won't need to replace that for a while* ... But with this car it was always, *Oh God, what've they done now?*

There were parts installed without seals, wires going to nowhere, glow plugs snapped off in the engine head. It appeared that when they couldn't get something working (which was most of the time) they had a tendency to ... well, I won't go into the mechanics of it, but in spirit it recalled a former housemate who, when the bowls of half-eaten porridge in her room started developing mould, tried to solve the problem by covering them in Glad Wrap.

With equal parts relief and dismay, I realised I was not the worst thing to have happened to this car.

The repair manual and the wiring diagrams kept talking about an 'RFW' switch, which was integral to the whole thing and which we couldn't find anywhere.

Then, one night, I jerked awake. Like a good detective, I had begun to understand the mind of my adversary. I crept outside with a torch and discovered that, after trying and failing to get the switching system working, the previous owner had screwed a radio over the top of it. I unscrewed the radio, and nestled underneath it was the switch, with the letters 'RFW'. I began spluttering. 'You just ... you just don't treat a car like that. Have some respect!'

There was still one job to do (not counting the long list of other jobs that I was trying not to think about): I had to change out a warning light on the dash. Decades ago, my dad had gone bush with a 1969 Toyota LandCruiser. It was designed so that you could take the whole thing apart with a 14-millimetre spanner. There was so much room, he said, that you could practically stand in the engine bay while you were working on it.

By contrast, judging by the repair manual, to change a light in this car's dashboard was going to take about six hours. I would have to take off all the trim, remove the stereo system, disassemble the steering wheel ...

I was so philosophically opposed to the job that I was beset with a great weariness. I could barely hold the spanner. My dad came in and found me catatonic on the couch.

'You have to disassemble the steering wheel?' he said. 'What a load of bullshit.'

He disappeared into his shed and came back twenty minutes later with a jerry-rigged replacement.

'Here you are,' he said, 'when this is on, you're good to go.'

*

After hugging my parents goodbye, I turned onto the familiar highway – that long stretch of road connecting my family to my friends.

I came down from the Adelaide Hills in a long, sweeping curve. The car was loaded with tools. As long as one of three very specific things went wrong then I would be able to fix it, but for now it was running beautifully. The borders had lifted, and a trickle of traffic was coming from the other direction. The roads were open. And shrunken dreams could spread out once again across the plains.

# 10

# I Fought the Law

I received a letter from a government department that read, 'You have been overpaid by $1314.' The letter was unsigned. At the bottom it merely said:

**Director, Earned Income**
**Customer Compliance**

I didn't feel like someone who'd been overpaid. When the letter arrived I was living in a van with towels strung up everywhere to cover the windows. It wasn't even my van. The letter (a digital letter – creepily, they would always arrive in the middle of the night) said that I had thirty days to pay. I began, quietly, to seethe.

The letter gave no explanation for how the debt was calculated, provided no evidence of any kind. This, I came to discover, is because it was a stab in the dark.

My job at the time was hammering wood. I would get two pieces of wood from the shelf and nail them together. Then I'd find two more pieces, and so on. Normally it was a little on the dull side. But on the day of the letter I bashed away with the fury of Thor. No force of nature will ever separate the pieces I hammered together that day.

The next day I tried three times to get the department in question – Centrelink – on the phone, but no luck. And no surprise. In 2013/14, Centrelink kept Australians waiting on hold for a combined 143 years. And that's just counting the time for people who got through. Despite never mastering their own telephone system, the department's officials nevertheless strode boldly into the murky world of data matching. And they were using it to send out debt letters galore.

In their initial letter to me, they pointed to the difference between my reported earnings for 2017 and their own data-matched figures, as if to say, *How do you explain THIS?* At first I misunderstood. I thought they were asking me to explain how *they* had got it wrong. 'Oh God,' I said, 'with pleasure', and sent them a detailed explanation by post. It did not seem to have done the trick.

So, robodebt letter in hand, I tried calling again and waited on hold. Finally someone picked up.

I tried to explain that they'd made a mistake.

The compliance officer said, 'We understand that the ATO-matched data isn't always accurate —'

'Oh, thank God.'

'We understand that the ATO-matched data isn't —'

'So, that's that, then.'

'We understand that the ATO-matched data isn't always accurate,' the compliance officer said again, 'which is why we give you the opportunity to appeal your case.'

What happened to just getting mugged? Those were the days.

The flaw in their maths was so basic, so fundamental, that I found it almost impossible to explain. It was like trying to explain walking.

'Well, if you haven't done anything wrong,' said the officer, 'then there won't be a problem.'

Imagine having to prove for insurance purposes that your wife is not a dolphin. And no matter how many photos you provide of her doing chin-ups and playing video games with her thumbs, the insurance company keeps saying, 'Yes, but then why did she visit Sea World?'

I spent days and weeks on the phone with Centrelink. Even when I tried to play it cool I'd somehow end up shrieking down the phone line. Being right only made it worse, because it seemed to matter so little.

At this point in the story, it's probably necessary for me to explain the maths behind it all, to explain how the government was averaging out the incomes of people working casual or precarious jobs in a way that had no bearing on reality, and then using it as the basis to accuse them of owing debts.

You can follow along with a pen and paper. First, draw a picture of a rabbit with half its brain missing. Now imagine that you are being audited by the rabbit.

I began to suspect that no one at Centrelink was even *trying* to understand the maths. But I couldn't stop trying to explain it. It was like a madness. The same thing was happening at parties. Do you think this is the sort of sexy injustice you can regale people with at the dip table? It is not.

The whole thing sounded so *Soviet*. But I was surrounded by genial Australians saying, 'I can't imagine our government ever doing *that*.'

Eventually I called my old work, got all my old payslips, indexed them, highlighted pertinent sections and sent them to Centrelink with explanatory notes.

A few weeks later I received a notice saying that my revised debt was now $95.74.

Principles, as you may know, are a dumb basis on which to form an argument, especially if you care for such things as your sanity, your sense of humour or winning the argument.

I could have bought myself a lot of life if I'd just paid that $95. I could have spent whole days reading Chekhov in the sun. I could have had a love affair.

But the principle of it was so galling. If someone falsely accuses you of owing $1314, why would you suddenly believe them just because they tone it down a bit? Especially if they're still using the same bananas maths.

Winter was turning into spring. My football looked at me mournfully from the passenger seat, wanting to be kicked.

'Not today, buddy,' I said.

I persisted with phone calls. One Wednesday after-noon, I refused to get off the phone until someone could adequately explain the maths to me. It was the recourse of the desperate.

'It's too complicated to explain over the phone,' said the young guy miserably. We had been going for several hours now. 'I will send you the assessments by mail.'

'If you can't understand it, how am I going to?'

I hung on to the call. If they wanted my $95 they were going to have to earn it.

The guy said, 'Actually, sir, my shift finished twenty minutes ago,' which is how I finally got to speak to a supervisor.

The supervisor swaggered onto the phone.

'G'day,' he said, 'I hear you've been having some issues.'

'You could say that.'

The supervisor, Brent, said he'd look into the figures himself. Go over the whole thing top to bottom.

'If you haven't done anything wrong,' he said, 'then I'm sure there won't be a problem.'

'Yeah, yeah.'

My friend once gave me some mountain-biking advice. If an obstacle appears in your path, he said, don't look at it or you'll hit it. Focus, instead, on the gap. No matter how small, he said, go for the gap.

If I reach old age and decrepitude, will I look back on this as a worthy battle? Surely my old self would want, instead, to know: What did you do with your body when it was still young and limber? Did you ever run foolishly at full tilt through an open field? With whom did you laugh? Did you invent? Did you find some path through the trees? Or did you stand there donking your head against them in the name of justice?

The next day Brent, the supervisor, called and said, 'I've got some bad news for you, mate. Your debt is actually *more* than we thought it was.'

That was it for me; I was finished. I'd been fighting for too long. I wanted to curl up, suckle on a teat. And Brent's was the only teat around.

'Listen,' I said. 'Maybe I did make a mistake. How about I just pay the $95 and we call it even?'

'I can't do that,' said Brent. 'Once it's in the system, that's what it is.'

A week later, the assessments arrived at the house I was now living in. And finally, for the first time in the whole ordeal, things became funny. They had sent me black-and-white proof that I was not the crazy one. I clung to the papers like they were a life raft.

Their provisional assessment had come up with a figure of $177. Then, after doing their data matching, they came up with $1314. In the next assessment, they made a simple accounting error that had them owing *me* $1004. (I never got a midnight letter about that one.) Then it was a debt of $95.74. Then $216.26. And then, insanely, I was sent a final debt notice for $312, which was the total of the *last two assessments added together*.

That's funny! It's funny that the department doing this to people was called the human services department. Imagine if the roads department sent crews out to dig potholes. Or remove the middle of bridges. It's funny that entire call centres' worth of people were being paid (much more than anyone on welfare) to enforce debts that didn't exist. Viewed from some angles, it looked an awful lot like the government was running a welfare program for debt collectors.

I called them once more. A friendly lady on the phone said, 'Hmmm ... that doesn't sound right. I'll have a manager call you straight back.' That was the last I heard for six months. I assumed their silence was a sheepish one. That they had dropped the case. But then I filed my tax return, and was due to receive a modest refund. On the day it arrived I got an email from Centrelink saying that, per some regulation, they had gone ahead and taken the $312 plus interest straight out of my refund.

And that was pretty much checkmate.

Except you can't cure stubbornness that easily.

I put it to appeal one last time.

The government will say that it is cracking down on welfare fraud. They talk as though they've bred some sort of super-beagle for sniffing out welfare cheats. What they've really got is a sniffer dog that loses its mind every time it smells luggage. And the government has let them loose in an airport where four hundred thousand people are trying to make their flights.

One year after my first notice, I got a letter in the mail saying that their assessment (using the same bogus maths with which they accused so many others) had got it wrong, that I didn't owe anything, that a refund was on the way.

Well, shit. I tried to tell them.

# 11

# Always Coming Home

I was supposed to be writing a book, which, it turns out, is a lot harder than reading one. I had chosen a room in the middle of Hanoi's Old Quarter because I love the inconvenience of narrow streets, especially winding ones: they make you feel better about not rushing off in straight lines all the time.

The room was on the fourth floor. It had a single barred window that afforded you all the sounds of Hanoi without bothering you with its sights. The bars added a nice menacing touch. Every time I gazed out the window and contemplated having a love affair, they seemed to growl at me, reminding me to get serious – not just about the book, but about life.

*

Through some sort of misunderstanding, Hanoi seemed to be in the grip of a proper winter. People were wearing jackets. Pants, even. At first I tried to endure it, but the cold kept seeping into my 'new perspective on things', so I went splashing through the Old Quarter looking for a jacket.

I stayed in Hanoi for two weeks. I spent mornings working in the hotel. Up came the sounds of beeping horns, birds and the wanton hammering of the hardware precinct. Occasionally, the smell of fresh bread drifted through the window into the room, where I was busy trying not to drown myself in the tub.

At lunchtimes I came bounding out of the hotel, freed at last from the seriousness of my room, to go searching the streets for bun cha, a meal of fragrant herbs, noodles and caramelised meatballs floating in a sweet, tangy, complex sauce that wasn't serious at all, merely magnificent.

Families piled onto scooters. People wheeled bicycles loaded with dried fish or bananas. In the evenings, two ladies squatted on the corner and, in a ritual I didn't understand but could sympathise with, set fire to a small pile of lottery tickets.

*

When travelling, there's always the distant hope that you'll find the place you belong. Maybe you'll come across a remote village in which you still suffer from hayfever but where sneezing is seen as a sign of virility. Or you'll have the opportunity to lead some town out of crisis and become their beloved mayor.

I travelled down the coast as far as Hoi An, but everyone seemed to be getting on fine without me. Only the book needed my help.

I stayed in port towns and fishing villages whose industriousness failed to wear off on me. In Hoi An, I spent most of my mental energy trying not to buy a three-piece suit. One day, walking along the river, I had a sudden urge to drink beer with the old fishermen but remembered with swooping sadness that (a) I'd never bothered to learn Vietnamese, and (b) I was supposed to be indoors writing the book.

From nearby Da Nang I went north again and caught a train along the Hai Van Pass. Below us, a mat of trees and vines climbed the slope from the ocean up to where our train was gingerly picking its way around the curves.

Phong Nha is known among tourists as the adventure capital of Vietnam, but I forswore the caving, kayaking and hiking in order to continue the important business of sitting at the dresser and checking my reflection to see if it was getting any work done. On my 'breaks' I sat on my bungalow's balcony overlooking rice paddies and watched a blue kingfisher, who was watching the small pond below us, which was teeming with fish. The fish, at least, looked to be having the time of their lives.

At the start of a trip, you have a whole block of time. Before departure, you imagine it in different shades and colours. The first few days nibble away at the edges of it. The next time you look, it's half gone. Then you notice with rising alarm that every time you look it halves, and halves again.

I had one more stop before flying home. I got off the bus and hiked for 7 kilometres or so, following a river in the direction of Ninh Binh. My backpack, which I had hoped might have acquired the heft of a manuscript by now, or some other meaningful weight, bounced around and chafed my sweaty shoulders.

I followed the river and then turned onto a road along which small shops, villas and restaurants started to appear. It was grey and drizzling. The road took me along a canal and through a small township. I kept walking. When I came to the end of the road, I turned left and followed a goat track past a rice paddy, a vegetable patch and a dog that was tied up and barking at the end of his tether. The track skirted the edge of a large pond, and then it, too, came to a stop at the base of a sheer limestone wall. In the shadow of the cliff, my bamboo hut jutted over the pond.

As I walked inside and saw the carefully made-up bed, the tender light fitting, I remembered with a wild panic how much I hate huts. The problem with huts (and their rich cousin, the studio apartment) is that there aren't even rooms to travel between. You just sit there with all of your things, which look at you as if to say, *What now?*

Outside, a duck quacked incessantly.

One of the purported benefits of travel is that by leaving behind your friends, family and possessions (except the ones that will fit in your rucksack), you gain the opportunity to find out what you're really made of. But I *like* my friends. How did I keep ending up so far away from them?

I will spare you the details of what went on in the hut. But I was there.

On my last day, I went poking around the village. Halfway up the local hill, I bumped into a pair of goats who were grazing by the edge of the path. I reached out and tried to pat one of them on the rump. She took off in a bleating panic. But even as she fled for her life, she continued tearing leaves off passing bushes and munching them down mid-flight. I marvelled at her: What appetite! What joie de vivre!

I turned and looked across the plain. Carefully tended rice fields stretched out to a river, which wound its way between squat limestone mountains. Soft rain moved in sheets across the valley. And it was all wasted on me. I would be returning empty-handed. I had failed to fulfil my mission, and had not, in the process, even had much fun. Through a complex series of mental gymnastics, I had somehow managed to achieve the worst of both worlds.

*

Avalon Airport is a single-runway airport in the middle of a paddock, about one hour south-west of Melbourne.

My plane landed at 8.55 a.m. I was dazed, groggy, had barely slept on the flight. The skies above the tarmac seemed huge. I blinked in the sunlight. As I dragged my bag towards the terminal, I stopped, looked up, and thought, *That is a great-looking shed.*

Sometimes you have to leave, but now I had returned.

Inside, the building was too small to impose its whole world on you. No matter what anyone said or did, sunlight kept pouring in through the doors, windows, skylights.

At immigration I could barely concentrate on the questions they were asking; I could just feel that sun coming in through the windows. My answers, whatever they were, must not have agreed with the immigration officer. She wrote something on my re-entry card and I was pulled aside by a young, bohemian-looking man from Border Patrol. He was affable, had nice eyes – in a different world we might have been friends.

'Vietnam, hey?' he said. 'What were you doing over there? Were you on holidays, or ... '

I didn't want to tell him about the soul-searching, so I gave the next truest answer: 'Hanging around, I guess.'

He looked at me. 'What would you say were your favourite places over there?'

My brain just kept repeating the things he was saying, 'Favourite places ... favourite places ...' For some reason I couldn't think of a single place I'd been to. I was dimly aware that this might be a problem. But I didn't feel like a single man trying to pass through customs. I felt like a river flowing towards the sea. No matter what they put in my way I would flow around it effortlessly and out through the gates.

'Well, I guess that depends on what you mean by favourite.'

I had purchased nothing in Vietnam other than what I'd eaten. My feet had barely touched the ground. Immigration-wise, I was guiltless.

The Border Patrol guy looked at me, harder this time. He knew something was up, but he would never know what. This whole thing – immigration, border control – seemed as insignificant as a Lego kingdom built on a kitchen floor. For a moment, I knew the feeling of pushing up through warm dirt with all the other grass. I knew what it was like to be a shoal of fish.

As I walked towards the gates and the sunny morning, the Border Patrol guy tried one last time.

'Did you bring any cigarettes? Drugs?'

This time I chuckled. I appreciated his efforts.

I turned around and said, 'Nah.' But inside I was all the leaves of home, rustling in the wind.

# PART THREE

# 12

# The Art of Tour Guiding

**M**elbourne drifted into autumn. The endless dusks of summer faded into cool nights. And I was wasting the best years of my life arguing with the phone company (with whom, I forgot to mention, I was also embroiled in a bitter dispute). I dreamed of making babies – hundreds of them – to help carry on the feud. It would be our family call centre versus the phone company's.

Instead, I took up my old trade: tour guiding.

Every time you think you're out ...

The tour guiding wage gave me a roof over my head (or at least, the lease on a portion of someone else's). The roof I didn't mind, but the walls! During my stint at the dog park I had grown accustomed to a certain quality of vista that was sadly lacking down my end of the rental market.

This time, I drove people down the Great Ocean Road, to Gariwerd (the Grampians) and Kangaroo Island. Almost as though I was skirting the edges of Central Australia, where I had learnt my trade, and which I missed so much.

Between tours I tended a little herb garden, gazed out the window at the brick wall opposite, and tried to make a good fist of civilised life.

*

Tour guiding in Australia is easy on some levels: you feed your charges well, take them to the right places and try to keep their feet warm. But extreme weather, mechanical problems, flies in the daytime, mosquitoes at night, the Germans, the lack of sleep, the feelings of deep existential loneliness ... all these things will conspire against you.

You should never, or almost never, give your tourists the choice of two options. This is a mistake inexperienced guides often make. Are you not the leader of this expedition? Have you not been here a hundred times before and know what it's about? Don't go inflicting the misery of democracy on them. It may seem generous and noble, but in the middle of an Australian summer I have seen people reduced to tears.

An outback tour is not a luxury cruise. A cruise liner gives the impression that everything is taken care of, and available. This is impossible when you're the sole driver/guide, and it doesn't make for a good experience anyway. I prefer to give the impression of barely contained chaos. It contributes to people's sense of adventure and togetherness. When it's going well, it feels like you're the captain of a pirate ship.

If a family of native mice sneak on board your bus and are only discovered when you're barrelling down the highway, don't stop. If there is screaming and hopping and running about, smile ruefully and say, 'Welcome to the outback.' This is the most important phrase in your arsenal. Keep driving if you can. Maybe shout some words of encouragement as the tourists round up the mice into saucepans.

On the first day of a Central Australian tour that I regularly ran, someone would always ask what time we were going to arrive at camp. Because camp was 600 kilometres away, it was a good opportunity to set a few things straight.

'Look,' I'd say, 'this isn't the Deutsche Bahn. There are rogue cows, flat tyres, and headwinds like you wouldn't believe.' I'd stare wistfully out the window for a moment. 'In some ways we'll be lucky to get there at all.'

I tried to leave it at that one morning, but the girl who asked the question kept looking at me expectantly.

I sighed. 'What time? I dunno. About 6.30, 7?'

'Okay! Thank you!' She turned to her friend. 'He says we're arriving at 6.37.'

A tour guide should try not to say too much on the first day. A week is a long time, and you don't want to devalue your own currency. By the end of a tour, no one remembers the first day anyway. Put some music on and start driving.

An older guide once said to me, 'It's like cards. Don't throw all your aces down on the table at once. You gotta play them one at a time.' (This is bad advice for actual card games.)

A critical job for any tour guide is to bond the group. You want them to feel as though, for the next six days, they're all part of the same adventure. My favourite way to do this on an outback tour was to go bush camping. With the sun low and the cockatiels bursting from the trees, we'd go plunketing down some dirt track.

When we stopped in a clearing and turned off the engine, sometimes there'd be confusion.

'But there is *nothing*.'

'Isn't it wonderful?'

Bush camping worked for many reasons, chief among them that no one wants to die alone. The tourists would come out of the bus in small groups and look around. Strangers would go off to pee together and come back friends, or scatter in twos and threes to collect firewood, and get bitten by ants. I watched it all proudly from the top of the trailer.

There'd be a German guy saying, 'Don't you have a chainsaw? For making the firewood?'

'Hell no!'

Sometimes I hid the matches, to make it even more fun for them.

Those were always the best nights. We drank beer and cooked chicken on the fire, with the Milky Way smeared across the black sky. People really started talking, and slept closer to one another than on any other night.

There are other ways of getting a group together, of course. I know a guide who, if he sensed malaise, would fake a flat battery and make everyone get out and push-start the bus. Getting bogged works, too, and having everyone dig the bus out with salad bowls. I once thought of fixing a radiator leak with Blu Tack, but didn't have any Blu Tack, so I passed around packets of chewing gum. If you can get twenty-one people all chewing gum for a common cause, what you have is a family.

Most tourists book the tour to see Uluru, but it's the experiences in between that really make the trip memorable. Your job is to provide the context in which a tourist can enjoy or appreciate them. Take Coober Pedy, for instance. Some guides treat it with disdain, or like an overrated lunch spot – and their tourists inevitably go away feeling the same way.

The town itself looks like a dusty Hobbiton. It's a hot and sandy moonscape, an 'after' shot in a film about global warming. The first thing you see when you're coming into Coober Pedy from the south is a lone wind turbine resolutely not turning.

It can look like a dump, frankly, but I am inordinately fond of it, and that's contagious. Many houses have assorted junk piles in their front yards, which take on a majestic, rusted glow at sunset. People have built themselves terraced front yards from old car tyres. There is half a spaceship on the main street and a tree that appears to be made from scrap metal. The early miners built the tree for their kids, apparently, who complained about not having any decent trees to climb. Even when it was built, though, they could only climb it a few months of every year without getting second-degree burns on their hands and feet.

From Coober Pedy to Uluru–Kata Tjuta National Park is about 700 kilometres – not a lot by Australian standards, but enough of a drive to demoralise most international tourists. In these circumstances, try to surround yourself with good people up the front of the bus. If it doesn't happen by chance on the first day, suggest that swapping seats every morning is a company policy. Drink coffee, tell stories and eat apples like a fiend to stay awake.

There are signs up and down that highway with sage, big-lettered messages like 'POWERNAP NOW' or 'FEELING SLEEPY?' Those signs will make you indescribably angry. You have to try not to think about sleep at all, because it creeps up on you: you check in your mirror to make sure the swags are still tied down, you start thinking about your own swag and how comfortable it is, and suddenly you feel your eyelids drooping. Try to think only of very active things, like being chased by wolves or robbing a supermarket.

On the way to Uluru there's a mesa mountain called Mount Conner. It's a much more common formation, geologically speaking, than Uluru, which is why Uluru has its own airport and Mount Conner has two toilets and a barbecue. But Mount Conner stands majestically by itself on the desert plain, so it's often mistaken for the rock. (Some locals call it 'Fool-uru'.)

Everyone gets excited and goes reaching for their cameras because it's a good-looking mountain. One time, stopped in the car park, I explained that it wasn't Uluru yet, and I saw a Swiss couple put away their camera without even taking the photo. I was incensed. 'Guys, it's the same mountain! It's the same mountain it was thirty seconds ago when you were all in a tizzy about it!'

But people want the rock they paid for. You can't just go springing a mountain on people and expecting them to fall in love with it.

The last hour before sundown is a beautiful time in the outback, Uluru or no. A sudden aching softness comes to a landscape that just five minutes ago seemed barren and unrelenting. I always felt beers were important at a time like this because you wanted everyone to slow down for what was going on. You could tell the non-drinkers because they were impatient for something to happen, when in fact it was happening all around them: breezes stirring the desert oaks, lizards emerging from clumps of spinifex, colours changing and the whole sky deepening into night.

If I thought the tourists would benefit from a sense of occasion, I would tell them that they were standing on the very sand dune where William Gosse (a white guy) and his party first laid eyes on the rock. People liked that.

'But couldn't they have seen it from the sand dune just over there?'

There's always one.

'You raise a good point, sir.'

I never had qualms messing around with the European version of things. Most of the best places were just named after some guy. It would be a madness to stand in front of the rock, with its ancient and enduring history, which has stood on that plain for as long as there's been a plain, and talk about So-and-so Ayers who once governed South Australia and had certain hobbies.

*

One should never let facts dominate a story, because no one remembers facts anyway. The best tour guides will turn an explanation into a story that's entertaining even to someone who cares nothing for the subject matter.

Then you'd hear the spiels of other guides: 'Now, the canyon is made up of two types of sandstone: the Mereenie Sandstone, which is 400 million years old, and the Carmichael Sandstone, which is 360 million years old ... '

If there was ever a more boring sentence in the English language, I didn't finish reading it. No one's heard of the Mereenie or the Carmichael Sandstone. Furthermore, no one can properly imagine how old 400 million years is, or, for that matter, 360 million years. What are the tourists being offered that they can't get themselves with an encyclopedia and a tranquilliser dart?

You have to start early in the mornings. If you let the tourists sleep in and start the walks too late in the day, it will take them a whole day to recover from that heat. The desert is alive in the early mornings, more alive than most can imagine. As the morning goes on, the shadows shorten and the sun drains the colour from the trees. 11 a.m. brings the death of hope. There's no more birdsong, just the sounds of buzzing flies and sobbing. You explain this to your passengers well in advance; you want them to feel that they have made the choice (though there is no choice).

The other thing we did in the summertime was sneak people into the five-star hotel, and its pool. Shady trees, deckchairs, waiters delivering poolside cocktails – luxuries like that are wasted on the rich. I used to explain the layout of the place to my passengers and give everyone elaborate backstories to explain how such a raggedy bunch had come into enough money to afford a five-star hotel. Then I would drop them off in groups of twos and threes at various locations and staggered intervals. I'm not sure any of this was necessary, but it helped with the sense of occasion.

The Australian tourism industry is overrun with white bread and overcooked sausages. If you learn to cook healthily for twenty-one people, with a bit of panache, and without it looking like a bucket of slops, you will go a long way.

It almost (*almost*) doesn't matter what you show them during the day if you feed them well at night.

I always carried a packet of Tim Tams with me in case things got rough, the way a cop sleeps with a gun under his pillow.

German girls will commit heinous crimes for Nutella at breakfast time. Europeans, in general, will not eat white bread, and you shouldn't bother making them try. The smallest women from Taiwan and Korea will eat twice as much as any man. And although some Italian men might be incapable of opening a tin of tomatoes, they will nevertheless have strong and vocal opinions on how to make the bolognese. These should be ignored.

Some of my worst tour incidents were precipitated by struggles with over-extravagant (and complicated) meals. I still cringe to think about the night I made quails wrapped in sage and prosciutto and spent two hours trying to balance them over hot coals in a pot-belly stove. The problem was this: no one wants to see their guide running around like a desperate MasterChef contestant. It's unbecoming.

There is a subtle but important difference between taking care of your passengers and serving them. When they see you running around like I did with the quails, it feels like servitude. And in gaining a servant, they lose a leader. It can spoil a group. You're taking on expectations that can never be met, and they will resent you for it in ways they don't entirely understand. They will start blaming you for the flies, the weather, the mediocre sunsets.

Two days after the quail incident, I was still feeling the shame. And then, 40 kilometres out of Glendambo, I started smelling burning oil. It had already been a trip filled with mechanical problems: we'd blown a heater hose and had to swap buses; we'd had flat tyres and an air-conditioning system that wheezed like an emphysema patient trying to get out his last words. Our exhaust had broken in two places and was held together with an olive oil tin. I was trying to keep it all together. When I sniffed the oil I almost didn't stop – by this stage the tourists and I were engaged in high-level psychological warfare, and I didn't want to yield any more ground – but it did smell serious.

I got out and trudged down the back. The whole underside of the bus and the front of the trailer were sprayed in oil. I opened the engine block and it was carnage; like a Tarantino movie in black and white. But I could see exactly where the oil had come from: a big round hole that should have had a cap screwed over it. I knew this because I'd taken it off the night before to top up the oil. And now we'd lost all of it through the same hole. By some miracle, the cap was still sitting upside down on the engine block. I dropped the cover down over the engine block and cleared my throat.

The tourists looked at me with deep suspicion.

'Folks,' I said, 'we've got ourselves an oil leak.' (Which was technically true.) 'In the gasket region.' (Which was not.)

There were outraged groans. Someone threw his St Christopher's medal out the window.

'Now listen,' I said, holding up my hands, 'I'm pretty sure I can fix the leak.'

I was sure I could fix the leak, insofar as screwing the cap back on would pretty much do the trick.

We limped into Glendambo. While everyone was preparing lunch, I bought some oil and told them I was off to fix the leak. After topping it up, I parked the bus behind the roadhouse and sat there enjoying a quiet drink and reading *Moby-Dick*. I called one of my mechanic friends in Adelaide and asked her if she knew enough about gaskets to explain to me how I might pretend to have fixed one. Then I tastefully applied some engine grease to my face so it'd look like I'd been busy, and drove back around to the lunch spot. I was beeping the horn and hanging out the window: 'Guys, I fucking fixed it!' And it really felt like I had.

I can speak fluent German. I thought it would be a secret weapon, which I could use for good if I wanted to or evil if I needed to. In six years of tour guiding I almost never eavesdropped on anything interesting.

At Uluru sunsets there was a lot of 'Ja, I have been thinking the same thing! Why does he cut the tomatoes so thick at lunchtime? Sometimes they are thicker than the bread even!' What sounds like complaining is really just Germans having a good time. They love bonding over logistical mishaps. It can really kill a good story, though. You start off setting the scene, explaining how you were in Sydney this one time, caught in the rain because the bus was late, and suddenly the Germans are all falling about with laughter. 'I know, I know!' they say, with tears streaming down their faces. 'The buses are always late!'

At Uluru I was doing some paperwork outside the cultural centre. It was late afternoon, but hot still, and the flies were rallying in numbers. I was sipping a cold lemonade.

A German girl had been giving me grief for five days straight. Some people are just hard to live with.

She plonked herself down across the table from me and started staring at my drink. Her friend sat down too.

Without taking her eyes off my drink, the girl said to her friend, in German, 'Look at that drink.' Then she let out a little moan. 'Ooooooh, what would you give for a drink like that? I'd give anything for a drink like that.'

I was thinking, *Mate, what's wrong with you? They're $3.50 in the gift shop.*

But the moaning was making me uncomfortable, on account of its rising pitch.

I said, 'Listen, would you like the rest of my lemonade?'

She looked at me suddenly with wide eyes and clutched the drink with both hands. 'No, I couldn't. I shouldn't. Maybe I could ... ? Can I?'

Then, as she brought it to her mouth, she turned to her friend and said, in her native tongue, 'Wait. Do you think he's diseased?'

Something broke inside me that day. I jumped up and started screaming at her in German. I mentioned unmentionable things. I said, 'Holy Christ, after everything I've done for you today, after all the things, the sneaking you into the five-star pool at great personal risk, etc., now this?!'

She was pleasantly surprised.

'Oh! Why didn't you tell us? You're German! That's why you have such good ideas, like the pool!'

Usually I wouldn't let on until the fifth or sixth day, when we'd just got back from hiking and people were hot and exhausted and thinking of other things. I would plug the microphone in and start giving the spiel in German.

On the last night of our tour, we would cook up a big gourmet barbecue and have a candlelit dinner. Once everything was ready to go, I would hit the lights, plunging us into a darkness broken only by the flickering of candles, and then play Marvin Gaye.

The real difficulty in these circumstances was not the cooking of the dinner but the getting people to eat it. They all wanted to take photos of it: sometimes there'd be so many people jostling at the end of the table that there was no one left to photograph. Just me, sitting there like a schmuck, and a sixty-year-old French woman saying, 'I never did understand Facebook.'

On the last morning, we'd hike Watarrka (Kings Canyon) together. The group would climb to the top of 'Heart Attack Hill', essentially the final summit. They'd look back across the desert plains and feel – justifiably, in some respects – that they had survived a tour of the outback. And they'd feel they did it together. A long-distance tour is different from a day tour. The group takes on a character all of its own. Four hours later, we'd traipse out of the canyon, and though they wouldn't all be friends, everyone would have played their part.

It's only five hours from Kings Canyon to Alice Springs, but it was going to be a tough drive: we'd had a 5 a.m. start and hiked four hours in the heat. I got everyone going with the coffee and the French toast, which the French couple insisted was just toast, then snuck off into the bushes for a power nap. I told the group we'd pack up camp and hit the road by 11.30.

Next thing I knew, I woke up groggy and confused to the sound of the bus horn. Somehow it was 11.30 already, and I'd missed everything. I jumped up and ran back to camp. I was irritated that they were beeping the horn instead of doing anything useful. When I turned the corner I saw that they were all just sitting there on the bus. 'For the love of God, *guys*,' I started to yell, 'we've got to pack this place up!'

And then I saw the swags tied down on the roof. I walked into our hut, and everything was gone. The food boxes, the bags, the cooking equipment had all been packed into the trailer; the place was swept up and wiped down. It had never looked so good. They'd even scrubbed out the fridge. The only thing left in the place was a cup of fresh coffee with my name on it. They were beeping the horn because everything was done, it was taken care of, and all they needed was me.

# 13

# A Fisherman's Lament

C onditions were perfect for a fishing trip: I had just lost both my jobs. But it wasn't all good news. I had also been fined $1200 for speeding behind the wheel of a tour bus.

Once again, Hollywood was no help. I want to see a sequel to *Speed* where Sandra Bullock and Keanu Reeves traipse around trying to contest the traffic violations from the first movie.

I wrote a letter of appeal to the Expiation Notice Branch. It took them five months to respond. I don't know what they were doing during that time, but one thing they weren't doing was running their reply past a copyeditor. The prose was so garbled it took me an hour to figure out if I'd gotten off or not. I had not.

I was in Adelaide when I got the news, visiting for the holidays. After the initial howling period, I packed my dad's old truck with fishing rods and camping gear and pointed it towards Melbourne, muttering about revenge.

'What are you going to do,' asked my dad cheerfully, 'catch $1200 worth of fish?'

I sighed. 'If only it was really their fish to begin with.'

Revenge is so complicated these days.

*

While the fishing wasn't particularly meditative in those first few days, the driving was. If you drive fast enough (or too fast, according to the bus-fines people), it feels as though you can outrun anything. You can crest a hill and experience a moment's peace as a new landscape unfurls. Then, of course, it all catches up with you, which is why you see people like me pacing around in country towns, trying to scarf down two or three custard tarts at once.

I had two weeks left to run before they took away my licence, and I was going to drag out every minute of the drive. I had planned to catch my meals along the way. At the last minute, my mum – either mis-understanding the nature of the trip or not sharing my optimism – had slipped a giant salami in with my things. In the days to come it would ride next to me in the passenger seat, like a talisman that I could nibble at.

I drove out through the Adelaide Hills. On the road to Strathalbyn, mist drifted across paddocks and gathered around lone red gums. Parrots burst from the roadside scrub and flew away. I called my friend James and told him that since leaving the city, my thinking had become clearer. I could see a path forward: I would dedicate the rest of my life to winning back the bus fine.

There was a moment's silence. 'How long did you say you've been out of the city for?'

'Two hours.'

'... Maybe keep going for a bit.'

From the Wellington ferry I called him back, thinking maybe he'd misunderstood some of the finer details. Normally James is one of the best people to complain to. Sometimes he gets so riled up on your behalf that you end up trying to talk *him* down. But this time he wasn't biting.

'Listen,' he said. 'Where are you now?'

'Crossing the Murray.'

'Is it magnificent?'

The Murray River looked sick and sluggish this far downstream, as though it was using all its strength just to make it to sea. A distant jetskier buzzed around on top of it.

'I drank from it once,' I said.

That had been on my first ever fishing trip. I was fourteen years old. On one of our afternoon excursions I'd found myself standing waist-deep in the river, a dreamy kid in possession of one great fact: this was where our drinking water came from. Even though it was the colour of milky tea, I bent down and drank from it, almost defiantly, rather than wade ashore for my drink bottle.

'You were defending your one big fact,' said James.

'I became ... violently ill.'

\*

Once ashore, I drove south-east along the Coorong, as mallee dwindled into salt flats and the dirt on the shoulders of the road changed from light brown to bone white. I made camp between the north and south lagoons.

Fishing can take you to the most beautiful places –
fresh beaches at dawn, with pink skies and wheeling
gulls – and promptly ruin your enjoyment of them.
All that fussing about with knots and bait; the hassle
of catching something, the anxiety of not. Sometimes
I think the perfect fishing trip would be to arrive at
such a beach with your friends, only to realise that no
one has brought any fishing rods. Then what? This
is what we're too terrified to find out, which is why
someone always packs the rods.

*

From the fishes' point of view, my trip was a great success. I imagined them lining up in the channels and
gutters of surf beaches, awaiting my arrival. I was like
an idiot prince, making all the stops, throwing them
the best bait money could buy.

Huge onshore winds made even that difficult. ('If
only he'd throw it out a bit farther!')

I kept trundling along the coastline. The truck
was not capable of any great speeds. On the bitumen,
it could manage 80 kilometres an hour and wandered all over the road. But I loved the world-weary
calm with which she endured me getting bogged on

beaches, and the roaring spirit with which she got us out.

At 42 Mile Crossing I tried to tangle with the famed mulloway, but spent most of the time untangling my line. I staggered around in the face of the wind like a drunk. My casts were lucky to make it past the shoreline.

At Wrights Bay camp site I became something of a pariah. I had grown so sick of watching my tent battle in the wind that I had abandoned it to its fate and gone to the local pub. When I came back, the tent was still standing (or leaning), but several people came over to complain about the flapping. I spent the afternoon lying spread-eagled in the tent, trying to pin it down from the inside, thinking, *This again.*

Morale was low; the salami was running out.

\*

I met someone in the nick of time. After taking the back roads into Canunda National Park, I had set up camp and was sitting in my folding chair on the dirt road so I could watch the sun go down. I saw the silhouette of another person coming up the road towards me. My heart softened at the sight of him: he kept turning around to look at the sunset as though it was trying to tell him something. Just as I had my fishing rods, he had a large camera hanging from a shoulder strap.

As he came closer, I said, 'Salami?'

He gave it a good look. 'Not for me. I'll join you for a beer, though.'

He grabbed his chair and, as he sat down, I recognised the look in his eye.

'Is it love or the law?'

He flinched. 'Is it obvious?'

The sun went down but the evening glow carried on. We sat and talked and drank our beers.

He pointed to my truck.

'Are you ... *parked* there?'

'Bogged.'

He chuckled. 'I'll help you out tomorrow.'

\*

After that first fishing trip (the one cut short by me drinking Murray water) I became obsessed. I did my Year 10 work experience on a fishing boat. I would sit in the back of class tying knots.

At the time, I was the coxswain of the girls' quad sculls rowing team. (The coxswain is usually the smallest person on the boat: their job is to do some rudimentary steering and to shout encouragement at the rowers. The rowers' tolerance for this sort of thing varies.) At regattas, I would sit on the steps of West Lakes – while the rowers rigged the oars or whatever they did to prepare for the races – and catch almost comical amounts of bream with a handline. I was a much better fisherman then than I am now. With the wet fishing line between my fingers, I felt I was receiving transmissions from the underwater world: the gentle pull of the current, the picking of crabs, and the moment when a fish turned its head with the bait in its mouth and took off.

I knew I'd gone too far when, on the way to the starting line, they caught me trolling a lure out the back of the boat. The glares of all four rowers were upon me. I apologised profusely, but that, too, proved to be a misstep – delivered, as it was, through a megaphone at the 750-metre mark. And that, coupled with the belated onset of puberty, was the end of my career as a coxswain.

I went on fishing trips all over South Australia with my friend Tommy, who was five years older than me and could drive. We would plan fishing trips carefully around tide times and moon phases. As I got older we started planning them more around the opening hours of country pubs and, eventually, not at all.

*

I drove the long way out of Canunda National Park and caught mullet from the beaches. (I would only ever catch one a day before running straight back to the truck to cook it.)

I followed sand tracks through the dunes and began to experience the slow untangling of the mind. Like sinking into a warm bath, I was returning to the world. I no longer swung my head around at the sound of bird calls, because I was surrounded by them. My thoughts, if I had any, were free to amble around. There was no one slamming them up against a wall the moment they left your head and shaking them down.

*

As I crossed the state border into Victoria, I had the feeling I was being reeled in from a great distance. Slowly and inexorably. Masks were mandated on this side of the state line, which only increased the sense of foreboding. 'It's true,' I texted a friend, 'they are only a minor inconvenience . . . if you don't care about faces or fellowship or the possibilities of love.' Though it's also true I would have been a lot less upset if I'd been paying better attention to my dental hygiene.

I thrashed around a little on the Glenelg River and then followed the road to Portland. I had a dinner invitation waiting for me in Melbourne, and I was in charge of the fish. This one-mullet-a-day business wouldn't cut it anymore.

I drove onto the Portland breakwater and set up next to a large Lebanese family who were drinking tea, baiting hooks for the kids and playing music. The whole breakwater had a festive atmosphere. A school of King George whiting was moving up and down the breakwater, and everyone, including me, was catching them.

That night I camped in the hinterlands, and returned the next morning needing three more fish before I could show my face at the Melbourne dinner party. The Lebanese family had gone, and the breakwater had a more sombre atmosphere. By noon I had caught two fish, and needed just one more, but it had gone quiet. I was packing up to go home when an audience arrived. Two locals pulled up in a fancy four-wheel drive, drinking takeaway coffees and complaining about tourists. I have spent many years working with men (and a few women) who talk like this: like crabs waving their pincers at each other. Not so much a conversation as a butting of shells. They glanced over my way a few times, but I was feeling soft and meaty, and didn't want to join in.

I was in a good disguise. The truck was sufficiently beaten up and I had gone long enough without showering that they couldn't tell *where* I was from. I went to reel in and leave when my rod buckled under the dancing weight of a whiting, a big one. Under the gaze of the two men, I tried to stifle my whooping. (The missing fish! The feeding of the masses!) Inside, my heart was doing somersaults. Outside, crab face.

I swung the fish straight from the water into the truck and slammed the tailgate shut. Then I turned, gave something resembling a bow and said, 'Gentlemen, I take my leave.'

'Wanker.'

Then I hopped in the truck and headed for Melbourne.

It is a mystery to me why I keep returning. I merged into the great flow of traffic. There would be no more camping trips for a while. No more driving west across the plains, arriving on my parents' doorstep just before dinner and gathering my nieces and nephews into my arms. I would learn to love the state, which had after all given us the roads, the aqueduct and whatever else.

From the main road I caught a glimpse of the city, with its tall buildings standing like sentries, and the familiar grey cloud hanging over the bay.

I swerved off the main road and down to a little beach for one last hurrah. I baited the hooks with my last pilchard as the fish waited for me in deeper water ... but who was I kidding? I didn't want to catch them, I wanted to join them.

# The Dying Art of Hitchhiking

I stood outside Pakenham, a hopeful man, trying to hitch a ride from Melbourne to Sydney. I watched all the sensible people drive past. After two hours I was so sunburnt I looked embarrassed to be there. After five hours they were still roaring past, and when a car did finally swerve off the road to pick me up, like talkback radio it was filled with lunatics.

I'd had some experience hitchhiking already. One night in Adelaide I'd hitched a ride with a guy who was so high he couldn't find the gearstick. He kept lunging into empty space with his hand. Eventually we had to pull over so he could find it by the light of his phone.

'Once I've got it,' he said, 'I've got it for good. I'll just keep hanging on.'

He rummaged around for a while. Then he hung his head. 'Well, shit. I guess it's an automatic.'

I'd hitchhiked around New Zealand and, with surprising success, on the backs of bicycles on the way to a football match in Amsterdam.

I seem also to recall soliciting a piggyback ride up Adelaide's North Terrace one time, but my memories of the incident are vague. (I remember the man's neck, though, which smelt of leather couches and hot chips.)

Hitchhiking is no longer the business of ordinary citizens. You don't see highways dotted with people anymore, and truck drivers are generally too busy or too wary to change down through all those gears and stop.

That day outside Pakenham, there seemed to be some confusion about what I was even doing there. A few people driving past returned my thumbs up, which was nice but not helpful. Possibly they thought I'd been positioned there just to give general encouragement to motorists.

Hundreds and then thousands of cars drove past. I stood on one foot. I stood on the other foot. I tried to catch my reflection in the windows of passing cars to make sure I was doing it right.

It has been suggested that the huge rise in car ownership means motorists have come to view anyone without a car with deep suspicion. *Who is this person,* they think, *and where is their automobile?* On a highway otherwise filled with cars, a hitchhiker looks like a weird, naked tortoise and no one wants to touch him.

I have only one friend who still hitchhikes, and I'm not sure I would pick him up. He has a big orange beard and hobbit pants, but he also has an accordion and gives the distinct impression that he's not afraid to use it. As their numbers shrink, hitchhikers become harder to identify with. You become less likely to take a gamble on someone like Jiffy.

I did some work for the local council once, interviewing cyclists and pedestrians about how they were getting along with one another on a certain shared boulevard in Southbank, Melbourne. Cyclists and pedestrians would come storming over.

'We need separate paths,' they'd say. 'One for the bikes, one for the pedestrians. We need a fence between the two. Maybe a wall. Write that down.

Does the council have money for a wall?'

It all sounded reasonable at first. But gradually, as the day wore on and the coffee wore off, they started to sound ridiculous. I mean, shit. You never see fish crashing into each other on the Great Barrier Reef, and here we are with brains the size of melons and we can't work it out? Dodging bikes and babies is how the brain gets its exercise.

When did we start relying on regulations instead of each other?

We forge these paths of convenience through our lives, as though the goal is to coast as smoothly as possible through to our final destination, unmarked by the world. But at what cost? Aren't we missing everything in our rush to a final destination which, in any case, is rushing towards us with equal speed?

Still, this *particular* car was a terrible idea. It almost hit me coming off the highway, for one thing. The car belonged to a man named Steve from Cheltenham, and it broke from the line of traffic and hurtled towards me. There were four people inside. Two of them were waving, none of the four was Steve.

The car skidded to a stop where I'd been standing. The boot sprang open, I threw in my rucksack, and someone yelled, 'Get in already!'

There wasn't much time for questions ('Are you sure there's room?', 'Is this really your car?' etc.). But after five and a half hours of waiting, you'd climb on a donkey if it smiled at you right.

I had one foot and most of my body in when we took off.

There were two guys in the front, a girl passed out against the window behind the driver and a big guy hunkered down next to her in the backseat. I squeezed in next to him and tried to make room for my feet among the whisky bottles.

He stared down at me and said, 'Stop moving around so much, city boy. You'll disturb the nits.'

I leaned forward. 'Hi! My name's Robert,' I said. 'Just thought I should, you know, introduce myself.'

The driver was looking at the big guy in the mirror and yelling, 'Your head's in the way! I can't see a fuckin' thing out the back window.'

And the big guy was saying, 'Well, look out the front one then,' which was advice the driver didn't seem to care for.

The girl woke up, said, 'You must be Dave,' and threw up in the ashtray.

We were up over a hundred in no time. Everyone in the car had been drinking, as far as I could tell, except maybe the driver, who had such a vague grasp on the laws of physics that it hardly made a difference. We were all over the highway. I'm not sure what he was doing up there, exactly, but steering was not one of those things.

Occasionally the big guy would lean forward and shout random names at the driver. After a time I realised he was shouting the names of the gentlemen on his whisky bottles, which made it slightly less confusing but no less disconcerting. Then he'd slump back in his seat and stare down at me the way a mountain might if it was stormy and just not in the mood.

He wanted to listen to music, so I gave him my headphones and played him ballads to try to calm him down.

Some argument started up between the girl and her boyfriend, who was in the front seat. We were doing about 120 when he climbed out the window. Only his curled white fingers and his legs from the knees down were still in the car, and he was trying to yell in through the window. Most of what he was yelling was being whipped away by the wind, so no one could really understand what he was saying or why he wasn't in the car anymore. We were all grabbing at him with both hands, trying to drag him back in. The car was driving itself, more or less, and it drove like a drunk. I could hear beeping horns and squealing tyres but had no idea where they were coming from. Neither did the driver.

'What the hell was that?' he kept saying.

We were coming up fast behind a caravan and lurching forwards and sideways trying to get around it. There was a B-double truck to our right, blocking us in, so our driver swung left and tried overtaking on the gravel shoulder. We clattered past the caravan. Gravel pinged off the windows and someone yelled out, 'Watch the paint job!' and then we were back on the bitumen ahead of the caravan and the driver turned around and said, 'So where you want us to take you?'

I looked down and saw my pants were wet from sweaty handprints. Only two of the handprints were mine.

'You know what? Here's fine.'

'What the hell?' someone said. 'We're not good enough for you now?'

The driver, indignantly, threw his hands in the air.

'You don't just turn down an offer of friendship like that,' he said. 'Where are you *going* to?'

I didn't know the name of the next town. Thinking about it, I didn't know the names of any towns between Melbourne and Sydney. I looked out the window for a sign, from God, the local council, anybody.

Finding nothing, I said, 'Just the next town. Whatever it is.'

'You said you were going to Sydney,' said the driver.

'I am. It's just ... I have to eat a chicken parmigiana in every town along the way. For this thing I'm writing ...'

The big guy was looking at me hard.

'I really love chicken parmigiana,' I said.

They thought about it for a while, or seemed to, then the driver said, 'Well, fuck you, city boy. We're taking you to Sydney.'


I have good hitchhiking stories, but good hitchhiking stories, like happy families, are all alike, and generally not much fun to listen to. This is why you won't see a new *Wolf Creek* film where a German couple get a ride to the beach with a friendly local and have a lovely time.

I saw *Wolf Creek 2* a few weeks ago. Sure, they succeeded in making hitchhiking look scary, but when we walked out I wasn't just afraid of strangers. I was afraid of wolves and creeks and cinemas and the woman I went there with.

In the car, there was some argument, started by me, about whether we should stop for more booze. At the last possible moment, the driver wrenched the wheel, and we went barrelling into the turn-off at 80 kilometres an hour. Another car was waiting to turn onto the highway. We came at them hard and fast. We hit the traffic island and launched into the air, straight at their flank, like a tiger leaping for the belly of a buffalo.

I braced myself against the seat in front of me. Finally, with everything rushing at us through the window, I thought, *Here might be a way out of this thing.*

Then we hit.

A pole between the two cars took most of the blow. I couldn't see the people in the other car, but that pole, I suppose, was the difference between ruining their day and ruining their lives.

The cars smashed into each other. The pole buckled. Our car spun around and started rolling down the side road, away from the highway.

There was a whoosh, and huge balls of flame erupted from the engine, which I thought only happened in the movies. I tried yelling sensible things from the back seat, but they came out sounding small and ridiculous.

I got my door open, trying to time a jump. All this I'd learnt from the movies. The girl was trying to get her door open too. She was scrabbling around for the handle and saying things that I couldn't understand. The car was on fire, and no one really knew how to behave.

But the driver was a new man. He took control of the car for the first time in the whole trip. He hit the accelerator, and we fishtailed away from the accident scene down the side road. The flames went out, somehow. The front of the car was black and smouldering. Some way from the highway now, we turned off the side road onto a dirt track.

The car stopped dead. Eucalypts lined the side of the track, and the afternoon sun came slanting in through their branches. We all got out, and the others swarmed angrily around the car. I snuck around to the boot and tried to get my things. The boot had been buckled by the impact and would only open halfway, so I had to tug away at the rucksack. When it burst free, I turned around and bumped straight into the big guy.

Something had gone wrong with his eyes. It was like seeing an empty cage at the zoo with the cage door still swinging on its hinges.

'Man, I'm gonna slice you up,' he said.

He started pushing me towards the shrubs on the other side of the road.

'I'm gonna slice you up and throw bits of you into those blackberry bushes.'

My bag was heavy on my back. I thought about running, but also thought it would simplify things in a dangerous way.

I stood there with my hands in the air. 'Hey.'

Our brains are funny things. On that dirt road in rural Victoria I had no good plans for escape, but I had fifteen years of education, and I kept thinking, *Those are* raspberry *bushes, aren't they?*

The big guy prodded me in the chest.

'Money,' he said.

I tried to sound cheerful, like it was my idea.

'I could give you some petrol money!'

I fumbled for my wallet and gave him $60, which was all I had. My hands were shaking. His were not.

'The cards too.'

I was stubborn about the cards.

The rigamarole of getting replacement bank cards in those days was enough to make you take your chances.

'You've got the money,' I said.

'You don't think I can use a bank card, is that it?'

He roared, suddenly, and went for the boot of the car. He was shouting about being just as white collar as anybody else and other disturbing things like, 'Where's my fucking machete?'

He had the boot open and was flinging stuff around. I was backing away, still with everything in my rucksack weighing me down.

'Where is it?' he was yelling.

In retrospect, I would guess that his machete wasn't in there (if he had one at all), because everything in the boot belonged to Steve from Cheltenham. I didn't know any of that, of course, and I'm not sure it would have helped – the big guy would have been dangerous with a finger puppet. I kept backing away with my hands up, expecting him to turn around any moment with a curved blade glinting in the afternoon sun of the end of days.

There was no machete. He found something, though, and spun around to face me.

The last thing I noticed seemed really profound. Everything seems profound about crime if it happens to you. I stood there with all of my possessions, with the shadow of clouds on the lonely road. From the corner of my eye I noticed two small, dark shapes hanging in the bushes, and thought, *Well fuck me, they* are *blackberries. I'm about to be murdered by a botanist.*

Then he came at me with the tyre iron.

The other three saw him coming and ran to stop him. The two smaller guys were jumping all over him, trying to pull him down by the arms, leaping up to whack him on the back of the head. The big guy kept coming. The girl was bent over and screaming like a Hollywood movie, 'Run, you idiot, run!' and as the big guy wound up for a swing, I ran.

I made it to the side road with my bag thudding into my back. I kept looking over my shoulder, thinking I'd see them somehow round the corner in the car.

I half ran, half stumbled up the side road and made it back to the highway. I explained to the officer arriving at the accident who I was, more or less.

She was a cheerful country policewoman; she and everyone else stood around the crash like it was a cake sale. The first thing she said was 'You know hitchhiking's illegal, right?'

I sat down exhausted by the roadside. Someone tried to tell me about the bus.

'I know about the bus,' I said.

The policewoman drove me the rest of the way to Drouin. As we drove, she sipped her takeaway tea and peeked at the GPS.

'So, you left this morning at what time?'

'About 9 a.m.'

'Well, you made it ... 23 kilometres.' She winked. 'Have you considered jogging? Could be quicker.'

I checked into the local pub and crossed the road for a meal. The doors of the burger place jingled as I walked in. I ordered my meal, sat down in a plastic chair and started shaking all over. When that stopped, I stepped outside. The Latrobe Valley lay before me like two cupped hands, not all of it parcelled up and sold off. My friends were waiting for me in Sydney. I stood for a moment, suspended in the late sun of a summer afternoon. Some philosophies would have us try to remain there, motionless, holding nothing except the remarkable fact of our lives. But already the question had started forming – beginning faint and far away but growing louder and more insistent – of where to go, and how to get there.

**Robert Skinner** was born and raised on the Adelaide Plains. His writing appears frequently in *The Monthly* and has also been featured in *The Best Australian Essays, Best Australian Comedy Writing* and *Internazionale*. He currently lives in Melbourne, where he works in a bookshop and plays football at the lowest level.